Small Gardens

Small Gardens

Essential know-how and expert advice for gardening success

CONTENTS

Choosing a design and plants that fit your small space and suit the gardening conditions will allow you to maximize the dramatic effect.

MAKING AN IMPACT

Taking time to plan your outdoor space pays dividends and will help you transform your small space with a high-impact design. Think about how you want to use your space and the style of garden you would like to create, bearing in mind how much sun your plot receives and the soil conditions it offers. You can then put together a design and planting plan that suits your space perfectly, allowing you to create your own little patch of paradise.

GARDENING IN SMALL SPACES

There are many easy ways to make a garden, regardless of where you live or the size of your yard. Even a tiny balcony, courtyard, or windowsill can offer space for a few plants to call your own, where you can enjoy the flowers or the taste of a ripe tomato that you've grown yourself. Research also shows that plants help us relax and boost concentration levels, offering yet more reasons to green up your space.

This chic roof terrace, complete with stylish furniture, trees, and shrubs, shows small-space gardening at its best.

Pots of produce make a tiny garden on the steps leading up to a front door.

Planters filled with summer bedding plants and attached to the railings of this tiny balcony create a sea of color to enjoy inside and out.

WHERE CAN YOU MAKE A GARDEN?

There are no rules about how much space you need to make a garden, and some of the tiniest areas are home to the most beautiful designs. With just a few containers or a small patch of soil, you can grow a whole range of herbs, vegetables, fruits, flowering plants, and even large scrambling climbers that can scale a wall or fence. A courtyard or small yard allows space for more expansive designs; perhaps a meandering path through plant-filled borders or a dining table and chairs surrounded by easy-care pots of drought-tolerant shrubs such as bay or Japanese aralia (*Fatsia japonica*), together with a few seasonal blooms. The options are many, limited only by your imagination and, of course, the growing conditions your space offers.

Planting in beds, with just a few large pots of flowers, is an easy-care solution for a small garden.

TINY CITY YARDS

Transforming a small space into a beautiful garden is relatively easy. Those shaded by buildings or trees provide the perfect home for woodland plants that enjoy cool conditions, while spots that catch the morning or evening sun in summer are ideal for seating areas. Before you start designing your space, consider how much time you have for maintenance, and remember that pots and lawns are more demanding than plants in the ground. Also check your aspect and soil (see pp.16–17) to ensure your plant choices suit your site.

UP, UP, AND AWAY

Vertical spaces such as boundary fences and house walls can take gardening to a new level when planted with climbers such as clematis, hops, or a rose (see also pp.68–73). The beauty of these plants is that they take up very little ground space, allowing you to line a tiny garden with lush leaves and colorful flowers, while leaving room for a table and chairs from which to enjoy the surroundings. Climbers are best planted in the ground, where their roots can expand, and will take care of themselves for most of the year once established. A few wall pots or hanging baskets planted with seasonal flowers can offer colorful highlights when the climbers are not in bloom.

Pink petunias in wall pots and a golden hop have transformed this boundary fence.

OUT IN FRONT

Front yards are often small and may double as a parking space for a car or two, making them awkward to design. Nevertheless, you can include plants in the tiniest of spaces, using pots on the windowsills or planting a well-behaved climber in the ground and training it up the house wall. All plants reduce the risk of flooding during and after heavy rain, and are especially helpful in front yards where the run-off will gush into overstretched drains in the street, while picking up pollutants that can poison natural waterways farther down the line. You can even plant in parking spaces by using tough species such as thyme, bugleweed (*Ajuga reptans*), and creeping jenny (*Lysimachia nummularia*) in areas between two paved strips just wide enough for your car's wheels.

Large pots filled with climbers such as a potato vine (*Solanum laxum*) and seasonal flowers located on a rocky base make a stylish flood defense.

ADDING UP THE BENEFITS

Gardeners instinctively know that being outside in a plant-filled space, however small, makes them feel better, and research now backs up this idea with proof that nature can improve our mental and physical health. The insects and wildlife drawn to green environments also help improve our well-being, as well as theirs, and even a small pot of flowers on a balcony can provide valuable forage for bees and butterflies. Another benefit is that all plants, especially trees, help mitigate the effects of climate change, adding to the raft of good reasons to create a garden in the tiniest of places.

Trees and hedges help trap tiny pollution particles while acting as carbon sinks.

CREATING A HEALTHY ENVIRONMENT

Plants protect the environment in many ways. They absorb carbon dioxide (CO_2), one of the greenhouse gases responsible for climate change, in a process known as photosynthesis. They also release oxygen as a waste product of photosynthesis, which we and other animals breathe in, creating a perfectly balanced ecosystem. However, in a world where trees and plants are being destroyed to make way for buildings, roads, industry, and intensive farming, the environment is threatened by excesses of CO_2 and other air-borne pollutants. The good news is that by planting trees, shrubs, and flowering plants we can help reverse this trend. One tree will store large amounts of carbon, and even the soil it's growing in acts as a carbon sink, reducing pollution levels. Research by the Royal Horticultural Society in the UK also shows that hedges and trees can trap the tiny air pollutants emitted from vehicles, allowing those living close to busy streets to breathe more easily.

BOOSTING BIODIVERSITY

Including a range of different plant species, and providing supplementary food and water for wildlife, helps increase the biodiversity in a small space. The term "biodiversity" is used to describe all the living things on our planet, from tiny microorganisms in the soil to huge trees. It's important because we rely on many different plants and animals to sustain the food we eat and the air we breathe. For example, research shows that bees and other pollinators are responsible for about a third of the world's edible crops, while the microbes in the soil help plants absorb the nutrients they need. Our gardens act as environmental lifeguards, and with every toad we attract or butterfly we feed, we're contributing to our own welfare and that of every other living thing on Earth.

Planting nectar-rich flowers in tiny plots can help feed key pollinators such as bumblebees.

Many different crops, including cabbages, sweet corn, and zucchini, can be grown in a raised bed on a sunny patio.

GROWING YOUR OWN

One of the joys of having a small area to garden is the space it offers to grow a few herbs, salad leaves, tomatoes, and other compact crops. You only need a few pots to create an edible garden, and while your efforts may not make you self-sufficient, they will allow you to try varieties that you can't buy easily in stores. Another benefit is that growing your own food, even on a small scale, has a positive effect on the environment. The energy required to grow and transport crops is contributing to the climate crisis, while the pesticides and fertilizers used in industrialized agriculture pollute the land and waterways, so gardening using organic methods goes some way to reducing the impact.

Growing lettuce in a few pots on a patio or balcony can generate a crop of fresh leaves from late spring to fall.

MAKING SPACE TO SOCIALIZE AND UNWIND

An outdoor room in a small garden or on a balcony or roof terrace will offer you extra space for socializing with family and friends and provide a beautiful setting in which to relax. A raft of recent research studies show that being outside in a green space also helps boost our health, both mentally and physically, while a lack of exposure to nature, known as "nature deficit disorder," can exacerbate feelings of anxiety and depression, and even contribute to illnesses such as heart disease and cancer. The simple act of planting a flower in the soil can increase physical health, too, as the tiny microbes in the ground that we breathe in while gardening have been shown to increase our immunity to disease.

The act of gardening improves mental and physical well-being, while the microbes in soil can bolster the immune system.

TOP TIP AS RESEARCH SHOWS THAT JUST TWO HOURS SPENT IN A GREEN SPACE CAN IMPROVE YOUR FEELINGS OF WELL-BEING, TRY TO RELAX OR WORK IN YOUR GARDEN AS OFTEN AS YOU CAN TO BENEFIT. JUST LOOKING OUT AT PLANTS CAN HELP, SO PLACE YOUR SOFA OR WORKSPACE WHERE YOU CAN SEE YOUR GARDEN OR WINDOW BOXES.

GETTING THE BEST FROM YOUR SPACE

Before creating a new outdoor space, it's worth thinking about how you want to use it and which features you would like to include. In a small area, you may have to compromise on your "wants" and focus on "needs" to fit in the essentials, but there will always be room for some plants. Folding tables and chairs, and cupboards for tools and furnishings, help make the most of small spaces.

Make a small shed an attractive feature by surrounding it with plants.

Create a space for a small bistro table and chairs to enjoy your outdoor space whenever the weather allows.

STARTING POINTS

Consider first how you plan to use your space. A tiny balcony or roof terrace with no room for seating will be more of a living artwork, viewed primarily from inside your house or apartment, so bear that in mind when creating your design. A seating and dining area makes a garden feel more like a room, luring you outside, even during the cooler months. If you do intend to eat or entertain in your space, consider a patio with easy access from the kitchen. A productive garden also needs a water source to irrigate the crops.

CHILD'S PLAY

Designing a small space for young children can be challenging, with no space for play equipment or to kick a ball. Rather than buying plastic toys, use existing natural features, such as a tree large enough to make a natural climbing frame or support a swing. Tents make great playhouses and can be packed away in the evening to allow space for grown-up entertainment. The novelty of putting up a tent means that children rarely tire of them, too. Alternatively, you could build a raised hut on stilts, providing space for children—and adults—to camp out.

A mature tree provides a natural climbing frame for children, while offering cool shade beneath for a seating area.

A tiny pool and a raised bed packed with flowering plants will draw in a wide range of pollinators and other wildlife.

NATURE TRAIL

Features such as a small pool and pollen-rich planting can bring a small space to life when bees, butterflies, birds, and small creatures visit and animate your garden with their activities. Nature-watching is very relaxing and helps relieve the stresses of the day, while entertaining and educating children. Planting a wide range of different flower and shrub species and attracting wildlife into the garden is also a great way to increase biodiversity and help the environment (*see pp.10–11*).

The priority for the owners of this tiny balcony is to grow their own food.

ASSESSING YOUR SPACE

Having decided how you want to use your small garden, it's time to assess your space in more detail. Making a list of the features in your existing yard that you want to keep and those you wish to remove is a good start, while measuring the space's size and shape will tell you exactly what will fit into it, which is especially important if you are planning to include furniture. Also consider how much time, energy, and money you can put into your garden, so you can make a plan that will meet your needs and suit your lifestyle.

MAKE AN INVENTORY

The starting point for any new design is to assess what your current space has to offer and to consider what you can keep or repurpose. For example, a small shed that's in good condition may be worth retaining, even if it's not yet in the ideal place, and a lick of paint could make it more decorative. Broken paths may provide the materials to create an area of paving elsewhere in the garden, and healthy plants, or even those that need a good prune, can be moved and revitalized. Always think twice about removing a tree, as the environmental benefits of a mature one outweigh those of young saplings. Try leaving it for a year to see what it offers in terms of blossoms, leaf color, shade, and privacy before making a decision.

Remember that there is no "away" when you throw something out: it may go to a landfill, so try to reuse as much as possible, and advertise anything you don't want on a local recycling website.

Write down any features that you want to keep, perhaps for repurposing.

BE WORK WISE

Like any room in your home, gardens require some work to keep them looking beautiful, so think about how much time you have to take care of yours and check that you will be able to care for the features you have planned. For example, pots on a balcony will need to be watered and fed regularly if the plants are to thrive, and the floor will require sweeping to remove debris. A small garden will need less maintenance if you install a patio and path in muted colors that won't show the dirt, avoid the option of a lawn, and plant shrubs and perennial plants in the ground rather than in pots. This is because most long-lived plants, once established, rarely need watering or feeding if they are suited to your site (see p.16–17).

MEASURING UP

Before proceeding with a new design, whether it's for a roof terrace, a revamped flower border, or a small yard, first measure your space. Just measure the length, width, and the diagonals, then plot these dimensions on graph paper to create an outline of the space, or put them into an online design planner or app. If your space is an irregular shape, try using geometric forms, such as squares, rectangles, or circles for patios and lawns in the center of the plot, aligning them with the house, and use the uneven edges for your planting. This will create a more balanced design, while the planting around the sides will disguise the overall shape.

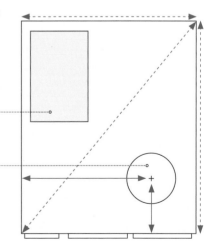

Take the dimensions of a feature, such as a shed, before plotting its position in relation to the three surrounding boundaries and the house

Use the house and boundary to measure the position of existing features such as trees

Plot the position of features that you plan to keep by taking measurements at 90° from the house and boundary.

Measuring your space's size and existing features such as steps is one of the first stages to creating a successful design.

CHECKING YOUR SITE AND SOIL

Identifying the type of soil you have will help you choose plants that enjoy your specific conditions. By checking for soils that are bone dry or become waterlogged after rain, and including plants adapted to these conditions, you can turn a potential problem into a beautiful feature. You will also need to assess the amount of sun that falls on the garden to help you to plan the best spots for seating and plants.

Your soil holds the key to which types of plant will thrive in your garden.

SUNNY SIDE UP

All plants need sunlight to live, but while some enjoy basking in bright light, those adapted to living near trees will prefer shade. Knowing where sunlight falls, and for how long, will help you choose plants suited to the space.

Standing with your back to your property, use a compass to see which direction it faces. Sites that face south will receive sun for most of the day in summer, while north-facing sites will be in shade. Those facing east or west will receive the most sun in the morning or evening respectively. Take into account trees and buildings that cast shade, and photograph the space at different times of the day and through the seasons, marking the areas of light and shade on an overhead plan.

You can then check the needs of your favorite plants by looking at their labels or information on nursery websites to see where they will thrive. If you have existing plants that you can't identify, their physical characteristics may offer clues as to their light needs. Many sun-lovers have small, silvery, or hairy leaves, and plants with colorful foliage or large flowers also tend to like sunny sites. Shade plants often produce dark green leaves with a large surface area adapted to absorb low levels of light.

IS YOUR SOIL ACIDIC?

The measure of a soil's acidity, neutrality, or alkalinity is known as its pH value. Most plants enjoy neutral to slightly acid conditions but some, including camellias and rhododendrons, grow well only in acid soils, while lavender and rock roses, among others, prefer alkaline soils. Catalogs tend to specify pH needs only when a plant is particularly demanding and you may find acid-lovers also listed as lime-hating or lime-intolerant. Kits for testing soil pH are very easy to use and will quickly identify your yard's soil type.

Rhododendrons prefer an acidic soil and their leaves will turn yellow when grown in alkaline conditions.

In the morning the west fence will be in sun

In the evening the west fence will be in shade

N

N

Morning

Noon

Evening

Morning

Noon

Evening

A north-facing yard will have shaded areas for much of the day, so locate trees where they will not rob you of sun.

In a south-facing yard the area directly in front of the rear fence will be in some shade for most of the day.

TESTING YOUR SOIL

Not all soils are identical and different types behave in different ways. Garden soils tend to be rich in either sand or clay particles, while some lucky gardeners have loam, which has the perfect proportion of both for good plant growth. However, there are many plants suited to each soil type, so there will be plenty to choose from.

Sandy soils consist of a relatively large particles, like the grains on a beach. Water drains quickly through the spaces between them, making these soils quite dry. They also tend to be infertile because plant nutrients, which are held in a solution of water, also drain away. Sandy soils are known as "light" because they are easy to dig.

Clay soils comprise tiny particles that trap moisture and plant nutrients between them. They are prone to waterlogging, and the surface becomes hard and cracks during prolonged dry spells. Termed "heavy" because they are difficult to dig, on the plus side clays are fertile and support many plants.

To check your soil, remove a small sample from just below the surface and roll it between your fingers.

Lavender, thyme, and salvias will thrive when planted in free-draining sandy soils.

Sandy soil, when rolled between your fingers, feels gritty and falls apart if you try to mold it into a ball or sausage shape. It is also generally pale in color and will quickly drain after heavy rain.

Clay soil feels smooth and dense and retains its shape when molded into a sausage shape or ball. Soils with a very high clay content will not break up, even when bent into a horseshoe shape.

IMPROVING YOUR SOIL

To improve the drainage of a heavy clay soil or the moisture-retention of a light sandy soil, apply an organic mulch by spreading a 2-in (5-cm) layer of well-rotted compost or manure over the soil in the fall if you have clay, or in spring if you have sand. Worms bring the organic matter down into the soil where it will bind clay particles into larger aggregates, creating bigger spaces between them to allow water to drain. It also coats sand particles, helping them retain more water and nutrients.

Spreading rotted compost or manure over the soil, known as a mulch, improves heavy clays and dry sands.

CHOOSING A STYLE

Whether you are creating a new design or updating an existing one, try making a mood board or list of the colors, plants, furniture, and sculpture that you like. You can then use these ideas to create a space that mirrors your personal style. So, if you like clean, simple interiors, then a formal contemporary design could be right for you, or if your home is filled with artifacts, ornaments, and bright colors, you may prefer an informal cottage garden or plant-packed tropical scheme. Take inspiration from the styles on these pages and let your imagination fly.

CLASSIC COTTAGE

Cottage gardens are loved for their jumble of plants and rustic gravel or brick paths weaving through beds packed with colorful flowers. These gardens rely on annual bedding plants in pots; climbing roses, clematis, jasmine, and honeysuckle; and perennial flowering plants such as delphiniums, lupins, and asters, as well as shrub roses. They can look a little lackluster in winter when the flowers fade, so add topiary or neat evergreen shrubs such as *Pittosporum tobira* to add structure and keep the interest going.

Evoking a traditional cottage style, the summer flowers jostle around the door in this beautiful small garden.

Large troughs allow space to grow peas, bush beans, herbs, flowers, and more in the smallest of spaces.

MODERN MEDITERRANEAN

Herbs such as thyme, rosemary, and lavender that hail from Mediterranean areas will thrive in a sun-drenched gravel garden. Try combining these shrubs with diminutive perennial plants such as Mexican fleabane (*Erigeron karvinskianus*), sea thrift (*Armeria maritima*), and stonecrops (*Sedum*) for a colorful garden that will be easy to maintain, since these drought-lovers rarely need watering once established. Use ½–¾-in (10–20-mm) grade gravels for areas that will be used as paths and thoroughfares, as they are easier to walk on than fine gravel or larger cobbles.

FEAST FOR ALL

You don't need a large yard to grow your own vegetables. Simply pack them into small, fertile beds or try the wide range of edibles designed for growing in pots on patios, balconies, and roof terraces. Mix your crops with colorful flowers such as wallflowers (*Erysimum cheiri*), French marigolds (*Tagetes patula*), and snapdragons (*Antirrhinum*) to lure in bees to pollinate fruiting vegetables, including cucumbers and zucchini.

Drought-tolerant plants such as thrift and sea campion in gravel beds offer an easy-care, small-space solution.

This elegant terrace combines formal elements such as neat clipped
hedges with a contemporary bench and glass screen.

Tiny city yards often enjoy a warm microclimate that lends itself to tender plants such as yuccas, ginger lilies, and begonias to create a tropical look. Some may even overwinter outside in the city.

TROPICAL RETREAT

Take inspiration from a tropical island retreat to transform your small city yard into a lush paradise. Pack your space with a collection of hardy palms such as *Trachycarpus fortunei*; spiky phormiums and yuccas; and colorful begonias, nasturtiums, and ginger lilies (*Hedychium*) for a blaze of summer color. Surround a patio with these beauties to create a junglelike ambience, and remember that the tender plants are best grown in pots in frost-prone areas, since they will need to be brought indoors from late fall to late spring.

CHIC MINIMALISM

For those who like a clean, uncluttered look and have little time to maintain a lawn and flowery borders, minimalist designs offer a perfect solution. Chic and stylish, these gardens focus on just a few key plants, such as Japanese maples (*Acer palmatum*), bamboos in raised beds, and evergreen shrubs in containers, including false aralia (*Fatsia japonica*), sweet box (*Sarcococca confusa*), and clipped Japanese holly (*Ilex crenata*). Modern furniture and a paved or timber floor, with gravel and pebbles for additional texture, complete the look.

Two beautiful acers shade this simple Asian-inspired city courtyard, which is both stylish and easy to maintain.

Pollen-rich flowers, a shallow pool-cum-bird bath, and trees for nesting offer a home for wildlife in this courtyard.

NATURE'S WAY

Make a small space into a wildlife sanctuary by planting pollen-rich flowers that bloom in succession from spring to fall, starting with tree blossoms and spring shrubs such as mahonia and viburnums, and continuing the foraging feast with alliums, hardy geraniums, foxgloves, catmint (*Nepeta*) and sedums (*Hylotelephium spectabile*). Add a water feature, a log pile, and bird feeders for a garden buzzing with life.

A tiny table and stools, a sofa, and annual flowers create a luxurious city balcony.

DESIGNED FOR COMFORT

Balconies may offer spectacular views, but space is always at a premium and their design needs careful thought. Buy compact furniture, and plant bedding in slim containers and lightweight pots that hook over the railings for summer color, with evergreen shrubs and bulbs offering interest in winter and spring.

Winding paths extend the journey
through a small space, making it feel larger
than it is, while large plants blur the
boundary lines and create a leafy oasis.

OPTIMIZING YOUR DESIGN

Take some tips from professional garden designers to optimize the use of your space and make it look and feel larger than it really is. Plants and screens can provide privacy and mask the boundaries, while winding paths will extend your journey through the space and offer different viewpoints to add interest en route. Color theory also plays a part in garden design, with hot hues fueling excitement and cool blues and greens delivering a calmer picture.

DESIGNING BOUNDARIES AND SCREENS

Beautiful walls and fences can be key to creating a unified design because they help frame the space and are usually visible all year round. The height and style of a boundary can also determine your privacy and light levels, while screens within the garden can be used to make the space feel bigger, as well as disguising sheds, garbage cans, and other eyesores, which can be tucked behind them.

Bold painted panels paired with simple green hedging create a graphic boundary for this small modern garden.

SIZE AND STYLE

The first factors to consider when choosing a boundary fence or wall are the height and style. A tall brick wall will create a sense of enclosure, trap heat, and may offer privacy, but it could also block valuable light if it's too high. You will also need to consider the legal height restrictions, which in most areas will be around 6½ft (2m). In front yards, a high fence or wall can conceal intruders at the door, so select one no taller than 3¼ft (1m), which will prevent passersby encroaching on your yard while still offering a clear view of doors and windows from the street.

Brick walls can create a beautiful framework and look especially pleasing if the materials match your house walls.

If you have an old wall that is in a poor state, consider repairing it with reclaimed bricks or stones, which may be a cheaper option than replacing it.

Timber fences can make decorative, affordable boundaries. To allow light to penetrate into small yards while still maintaining privacy where it is most needed, install tall panels around a patio or seating area and shorter fencing or see-through structures elsewhere. Another option is a 4–5-ft (1.2–1.5-m) fence topped with a trellis panel to enclose a courtyard or tiny space.

Hedges provide a more natural boundary but are wider than fencing or walls. Offering foliage color and texture, and perhaps flowers, too, they also provide a habitat for wildlife. Choose slow-growing hedging plants that won't get too big (see p.26). If you inherit a hedge that is larger than you want, consider reshaping or cutting it back rather than replacing it.

A low picket fence is a good option for a front yard, where taller structures can present a security risk.

TOP TIP CONSULT YOUR NEIGHBORS WHEN PUTTING UP A NEW FENCE OR WALL OR REPLACING AN OLD ONE. OFFERING THEM THE OPPORTUNITY TO SEE YOUR PLANS MAY HELP AVOID DISPUTES AND CREATE A BOUNDARY THAT WORKS FOR BOTH OF YOU.

Slatted fences that allow wind to pass through will protect small spaces in exposed sites.

DESIGN SOLUTIONS

Whatever type of structure you choose, use just one or two materials (see p.26) to create a unified look, which will make the garden appear more spacious. If you have inherited an assortment of different styles, try painting them all one color to produce a coordinated design. Traditional dark green or brown fences work well in small spaces as they blend easily into the planting, or, for a more contemporary look, try using blue, gray, or black. Applying stucco to a brick wall creates a smooth finish that can be painted in a color to suit your style. For a similar effect with a wooden fence, fix marine plywood to it in order to create a clean surface.

In windy sites, opt for open-weave or slatted fencing panels or a deciduous hedge, which allow air to pass through and are thus less likely to be blown down during a storm than solid structures.

INTERNAL SCREENS

Using screens within a small space to increase the feeling of space may sound counterintuitive, but this design trick can work well, particularly if you have a narrow plot or wish to disguise something. Installing a gateway between two screens a short distance from the end of the plot and using a focal point such as a sculpture or pot of flowers at the end of the yard

An internal trellis screen can be used to mask the view from the house of less decorative productive areas.

will fool the eye into thinking your space extends much farther than it does in reality. You can use the hidden area to store your garbage cans, bicycles, children's toys, or a compost bin.

Small town yards are often long and narrow, and here you can disguise the true size and make the space look bigger by dividing it with a trellis panel. Install a screen about halfway down the length, with an opening on one side. The semi-transparent trellis also allows you to create different areas for, say, a vegetable garden or play area, while letting light pass through it.

CHOOSING BOUNDARY MATERIALS

While buying a fence or wall can be expensive, opting for cheap materials is often a false economy, especially if their weak construction means your boundaries blow down during the first storm in the fall and have to be replaced. Choose the best quality you can afford and ensure fencing panels are installed to a high standard—reputable suppliers often recommend approved installers. A stone or brick wall will cost more than fencing and it must also be built on solid footings to ensure it's safe, so call in an experienced builder for any wall more than 3¼ft (1 m) in height.

Painting a wooden fence can add a layer of protection against rotting.

FENCING OPTIONS

When choosing timber fencing, check that the wood has Forest Stewardship Council (FSC) certification, which shows it is from a sustainably managed forest. Most fencing is made from softwood that has been either dip- or pressure-treated. While both of these chemical treatments help protect against decay and insect damage, pressure-treated wood, which is generally more expensive, will last longer without further applications of preservative. Look for guarantee times to see how long products are expected to last. Hardwood fencing panels have a long life without chemical treatments but they are usually more expensive.

Willow or hazel hurdles are a biodegradable option, best for internal screens or barriers not intended to last for more than a few years.

BRICKS AND STONE

Walls constructed from bricks or natural stone, while more expensive than fences, are good investments since they can last a lifetime. Bricks come in a range of colors and can have a rough or smooth texture; those intended for a garden wall must also be frost-proof. Reclaimed bricks are the most eco-friendly option and their weathered finish would suit the garden of a period house, but check that your supplier can guarantee they are suitable for exterior walls.

Boundaries made from natural stone sourced from a quarry or reclamation yard close to your home are ideal for small rural yards. However, stone is more expensive than bricks, and you will need a stonemason to construct a wall, pushing the costs up further.

Stone walls blend seamlessly into small spaces in rural settings, especially when made from local rock.

EASY-CARE HEDGES

Hedges make eco- and wildlife-friendly boundaries, but they are wider than other screens. For a small garden, ensure that you buy well-behaved, slow-growing plants that require just one trim each year. Good choices include evergreen yew (*Taxus baccata*) and Portuguese laurel (*Prunus lusitanica*), or deciduous hornbeam (*Carpinus betulus*) and beech (*Fagus*), which both retain their bronze dead leaves over winter. For a more informal boundary, opt for a wildlife hedge comprising a mix of any of the following: holly (*Ilex aquifolium*), hawthorn (*Crataegus*), hazel (*Corylus*), field maple (*Acer campestre*), wild rose (*Rosa rugosa*), and guelder rose (*Viburnum opulus*). Trim hedges only when birds will not be nesting, from late summer to early spring.

Copper beech makes a dark red hedge in summer and then takes on bronze tints during the winter months.

Pressure-treated softwood timber fencing offers an easy-care, neutral backdrop for an informal design.

EXTENDING THE PERSPECTIVE

Designing paths that create a longer journey through a space can make it seem larger, while terracing a slope will increase the illusion of space by taking the eye up or down, and provide more practical areas for seating or planting, too. You can use the same idea in a level yard or on a roof terrace by building an elevated deck or including raised beds or planters to play with the perspective and create impact.

A winding path takes the gaze from one side of the space to the other as you walk along, making it feel bigger.

DESIGNING PATHS

The routes through a small space determine how you perceive it. Creating a straight path from the house to the back of the plot will take you on the quickest route end to end and accentuate the small size. Making a path on a diagonal from one corner to another or creating a sinuous route will extend the journey and make a space feel bigger. If you opt for a winding path, create sweeping curves rather than a wiggly line, which will look fussy and be difficult to negotiate. Planting around a path keeps visitors on track and allows you to direct their gaze to features en route, such as plants, a seat, or a statue.

If the space doesn't lend itself to longer routes, another perspective trick is to create a straight path that narrows as it recedes from the house, making it look longer—again, planting on either side enhances the illusion.

A CHANGE OF LEVEL

Different levels in a space take the eye up or down, which makes it look bigger while creating hidden areas to explore, even in a small plot. If your yard slopes naturally, consider terracing it to create a series of level areas, which are more practical for seating. The retaining walls of the terraces will also give you a vertical surface to plant up. If you don't want the expense of moving soil and building walls, another solution is to erect a timber deck over a sloping area.

In yards with no natural level changes, you can dig out a sunken garden, if the water table is not too high—employ a surveyor to check this for you. Stepping down into a snug seating area will enhance even a tiny plot. Alternatively, step up, using raised platforms, decks, or planters to create higher levels for seating or plants, but check that any elevated feature will not compromise the privacy of your neighbors. This layered look also works well on roof terraces, where raised beds filled with lightweight growing media (see p.82) and plants will double as windbreaks around seating and dining areas.

> **TOP TIP** WIDE, DEEP STEPS FEEL SAFE, ALLOWING YOU TO ASCEND OR DESCEND COMFORTABLY TO ANOTHER LEVEL. AIM FOR A RISE OF NO MORE THAN 6 IN (15 CM) AND A MINIMUM TREAD OF 12 IN (30 CM).

Steps take you down to this tiny sunken seating area, which makes the most of the space.

Take advantage of all the space by using the area under a raised deck to store tools or a mower.

Broad timber steps extend the journey through this sloped plot to a raised seating area at the top.

DIRECTING THE FOCUS

As well as disguising the boundaries and extending the journey through your space, use a few landscaping tricks for the areas within your small space to make it look and feel larger. Directing the focus up to the sky or into the center of the space will deceive the eye into thinking the area is bigger than it is in reality, while offering more opportunities to increase the planting on props such as arches. Alternatively, borrow ideas from Japanese gardens, where the perception of the space is directed by carefully placed flowers and ornaments designed to catch the eye.

The mosaic floor of this small patio area pulls the focus down and into the center of the space.

The wooden arch at the entrance to this tiny courtyard takes the gaze up.

A colorful canopy pulls the focus toward the trees above it, creating a feeling of more space.

LOOK SKYWARD

While boundaries create a visual barrier around your space, the sky offers a view of infinite space. By using features that take the gaze up to this vast blue expanse you can deceive the brain into thinking the space is larger than its actual dimensions. Use flowering climbers such as clematis or roses (see pp.70–73) to scramble over a trellis screen, arch, or pergola and draw the focus upward; brightly colored or white blooms will catch the eye more than green foliage. Introduce hanging baskets filled with seasonal flowers in strategic spots to give your planting a lift, and make you look skyward.

Tall sculptures will have the same effect, or if you have the space, a tree will be even better, especially when in flower or bearing fruit (see pp.48–53). Bees, butterflies, and birds will attract the eye as they fly from bloom to bloom or eat the fall berries; pendent features hanging from branches will act as high points of focus on a permanent basis.

The detailed design of this circular patio distracts the eye from the boundaries in a tiny space.

FOCUS CENTER-STAGE

Drawing the eye away from the boundaries is another trick designers often employ in small spaces. A circular or square area of lawn, paving, or gravel in the middle of your space will pull the focus center-stage, especially if you wrap layers of planting around it to draw the eye in. A plant or pot in the center of a paved area will increase the allure, or use the space for a small table and chairs. Surrounding the seating with tall plants can also offer privacy from neighboring windows and create a protected area, perfect for relaxing.

Install a mirror at the end of the space to create the illusion of an outdoor room beyond.

ON REFLECTION

Using a weatherproof mirror, designed for outdoor use, will make your space appear larger, while also reflecting light into it. The best illusion can be created by attaching a long mirror to a back wall or fence, with its base at ground level and a path leading up to it; this will look as though the route continues on beyond the barrier. Alternatively, use a mirror at head height so that you look into it as you approach and see the garden reflected back. Disguise the edges with planting to complete the visual illusion and also to deter birds from flying at speed into the mirror; adding a hanging basket will also help avoid avian accidents.

IT'S ALL IN THE DETAIL

The tiny details in a garden draw the eye away from boundaries and increase the interest in a small space. Seasonal plants that pop up for just a few weeks each year make you stop and look down when they push through the soil. Try small species tulips such as the dainty 'Little Beauty' (*see also p.87*), which appear with a burst of color each spring and then die down in summer, followed by low-growing hardy geraniums that bloom in summer and late-season performers such as blue lily-turf (*Liriope muscari*), which looks like a grass for most of the year until an explosion of purple flower spikes transforms it in late summer.

Ornaments such as shells planted with houseleeks, a small willow sculpture, or even a little gnome if that's your style will also attract attention and slow the journey through the space, making it feel larger.

The tiny species tulip 'Little Beauty' makes an eye-catching addition to pots or alongside paths when it appears in spring.

SPACE TO RELAX

A seating area will maximize your use of your yard, balcony, or roof terrace, drawing you outside to relax and enjoy the fresh air and flowers. When planning one, first consider the various vantage points, assessing the areas that either give you the best views or trap the sun at key times of the day. Then create a level surface that can accommodate furniture that fits your budget and suits your style.

LOCATION, LOCATION, LOCATION

Look for sweet spots in your yard or on a roof terrace that afford the best views of the planting or the city skyline, which would make ideal areas for seating or dining. While dining areas are best sited within easy reach of the kitchen, other seating does not have to be near the house and could instead make the most of an area in morning or evening sun, which will offer soft light, ideal for relaxing. Areas flooded with midday sun may seem like good locations for seating but they can be uncomfortably hot in summer and will require some shading, while those in shade all day may be too cold for most of the year.

A sheltered circular patio is just the right size for a small folding bistro set.

THE RIGHT FIT

A common design mistake is to make a tiny patio for a tiny space. Problems soon become apparent when chairs slide off the paving into flowerbeds and the family feels hemmed in around a dining table squeezed into a tight corner. Regardless of the size of your yard, make sure your patio space will suit the furniture you have your eye on by taking measurements of tables and chairs to ensure they fit. Create a hard surface that's at least 6½ ft (2 m) wider and longer than a dining table to allow people to push their chairs back, and allow 18 in (45 cm) or more in front of seats or benches to provide access and an area to place your feet when you are sitting down.

An area close to a covered veranda next to the house provides a practical, accessible location for a dining table and chairs.

PATIO MATERIAL CHOICES

NATURAL STONE Durable and hard-wearing, natural stone is a good choice for patio paving and paths, but it is one of the most expensive options. Sandstone, limestone, slate, and granite are all natural stones, offering a choice of subtle colors and textures. They are also frost-resistant, but porous limestone can stain easily if not sealed after it is laid. Check with suppliers that your materials have been sourced ethically, too, and consider the carbon footprint of their extraction and delivery if they have traveled around the world to get to you.

RECONSTITUTED STONE Cheaper than most natural stone products, this type of paving is made from concrete or a combination of concrete and other materials. It creates a durable surface and you can choose from the huge range of colors, textures, and styles, many made to look like natural stone. However, concrete is a very polluting material, so it comes with a high carbon footprint. It is also not as frost-resistant as most natural stones or porcelain.

PORCELAIN An increasingly popular paving material, porcelain is made from clay fired at very high temperatures, which results in a durable product that's ideal for patios and paths. Porcelain tiles come in a wide choice of colors, textures, and styles and they can also be made to look like stone or wood. They are nonporous, which means they don't stain and are frost-resistant. However, porcelain is more difficult to install than natural stone, which pushes up the price.

DECKING AND TIMBER PRODUCTS

Decking is a relatively inexpensive and generally eco-friendly landscaping material. You can choose from a softwood deck made from pressure-treated boards (see p.26) or opt for more durable, and more expensive, hardwood. Whichever timber type you select, look for accreditation that proves it is from a sustainable, regulated source, such as the Forest Stewardship Council (FSC). You can also use reclaimed wood, but check that it has not been treated with creosote or chromated copper arsenate (CCA), both of which pose risks to human health, wildlife, and the environment and are now banned in most countries. Decking made from recycled plastic or a mix of plastic and wood chip is a nonslip option and more durable than most softwoods.

GRAVEL AND AGGREGATES One of the cheapest landscaping materials, gravel is easy to lay yourself and a practical solution for informal seating areas and paths, although most types are not recommended for dining areas or under deciduous trees. Choose gravel in a natural color, $\frac{1}{2}$in (10mm) in diameter, and with angular edges, which is easier to walk on than fine gravels or pebbles. Self-binding gravels can be used for dining areas and are made from aggregates of different sizes that form a permeable, weed-free surface when compacted.

Natural stone can last a lifetime but it is one of the most expensive options.

Porcelain is a versatile clay-based material, ideal for patios and paths.

Gravel is an easy-to-lay and affordable choice for an informal design.

USING COLOR

Colors not only enliven your outdoor space but can also influence your mood. Bright reds, oranges, and yellows engage our senses more than blues, greens, and mauves and may help stimulate ideas or conversation in an area designed for entertaining. Cooler, softer shades, meanwhile, allow our minds to rest and are ideal for spaces where you want to relax. In small gardens, colors can be used to extend the perspective or pick out focal points, but there are no hard and fast rules; part of the fun of designing your garden is experimenting with the hues you like best.

Using shades of the same color can produce beautiful effects, as pale hues jump out and darker hues recede.

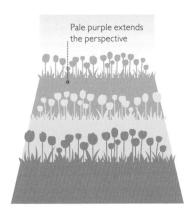

Pale purple extends the perspective

Hot reds close to the house and cool colors farther away help to make a garden look longer and more spacious.

Bright red jumps forward visually

Pale colors in the foreground and hot, saturated hues at the back of the space can make a garden look smaller.

COLORFUL PERSPECTIVES

Artists know the power of color to grab our attention or fade into the background, and gardeners can also use color theory to control the perception of space. Saturated hot reds and oranges appear to advance toward the viewer, while pale blues or greens recede. The effect is hard-wired into human perception because it reflects what occurs in natural landscapes, where the bluish haze caused by water and other particles in the atmosphere intensifies with distance, thus making colors fade toward the horizon.

This phenomenon can be used to make bold "statement" plantings. For example, surrounding hot-colored plants in a flowerbed with cool greens, purples, and pastel shades creates a strong focal point that will help direct a viewer's eye around your garden.

Before you commit to planting a small space, try moving colored cardboard panels, or even cut flowers, around the garden to assess the impact of hue on your design.

WHAT ABOUT WHITE?

White and cream are often used in small gardens to push light into gloomy corners, but they do not necessarily make spaces look bigger. Reflected white acts like a light shining onto a surface, highlighting it and bringing it forward visually, just as a spotlight on a stage will pick out the actors. In a flowerbed, a group of large white blooms can shout louder than the surrounding plants, and may attract too much attention in a mixed scheme. Smaller white or pale blooms have a more subtle effect, adding spots of light to brighten up your beds.

White will reflect light into a shady space but may be too dazzling.

Splashes of bold orange, tempered with cooler blues and greens, add excitement
to a small courtyard design.

PLANTING A
SMALL SPACE

Tiny courtyards, balconies, roof terraces, and windowsills offer a wealth of opportunities to employ the power of plants for year-round shows of color and texture. Discover how you can use a range of trees, shrubs, perennial flowers, and annual bedding in imaginative and surprising ways to create beautiful effects in your small garden. Training climbing plants such as roses and clematis up walls and fences will add another layer of interest to your design, while covering very little space on the ground.

CHOOSING PLANTS

The majority of plants can be used successfully in a small space, but it's always wise to do your homework before you buy. Select those that suit your site, soil, and the space available, which will allow them to thrive. Choices will be more limited on a balcony or roof terrace, where you also have to consider the combined weight of the container, soil, and plant to ensure your displays do not exceed the load-bearing capacity—if you're in doubt, a structural engineer can check that your structure will be safe.

The colorful half-hardy annuals surrounding this patio need full sun to thrive and will bloom for just one season.

UNDERSTANDING PLANTS

When buying plants, it's helpful to know a little about the different types and how they behave (see *opposite*). For example, in summer, you will find many flowering plants on sale and while some may live for many years, annuals and bedding plants sold primarily for container displays will bloom for only a few months before dying.

Woody-stemmed plants such as shrubs and trees create the backbone of a garden or container display, offering height and structure. Plant these before other types to establish a permanent framework. Evergreens keep their leaves all year round, while deciduous species lose their foliage over winter. However, while it's tempting to fill your garden with evergreens for consistent color, remember that deciduous plants often provide just as much interest, with early spring flowers, fall leaf color, and exposed textured stems in winter.

Many bulbs behave like deciduous perennials, but after flowering their top growth soon dies back. This means that spring bulbs will disappear beneath the ground when summer arrives, leaving a gap in your borders or pots until they pop back up the following spring.

Shade-loving hostas, euphorbias, ferns, and fringe cups (*Tellima*) will enjoy the cool conditions close to a tree.

RIGHT PLANT, RIGHT PLACE

The concept "right plant, right place" is the keystone of good gardening practice. Any experienced gardener will tell you that siting a sun-loving plant in a shady spot will produce poor results and may even lead to its early demise, so make sure yours suit your yard, terrace, or balcony by matching their needs with the conditions you can offer (see pp.16–17). Also take into account how much space a plant requires by checking its final height and spread. Plants grow throughout their lives and a small shrub may soon form a 6½ft (2m) specimen, so check the label or plant nursery websites carefully.

Tulip bulbs and annual bellis daisies are planted in the fall to create an explosion of color the following spring,.

PLANT GROUPS EXPLAINED

ANNUALS AND BIENNIALS Plants that germinate, flower, set seed, and die all in one year are known as annuals. Hardy annuals withstand frost, while tender types die when exposed to freezing temperatures. Biennials germinate and develop stems and leaves in their first year, then flower, set seed, and die in the second year.

PERENNIALS, GRASSES, AND FERNS Most perennials live for many years, but their top growth usually dies down in winter before emerging again the following spring; a few retain their leaves in winter. Grasses can be deciduous or evergreen and behave like perennials, while most bamboos are evergreen. Ferns are evergreen or deciduous and live for many years.

BULBS Plants that form bulblike structures, including corms, tubers, and rhizomes, as well as true bulbs, fall into

this group. They include spring-flowering daffodils, tulips, and alliums, which are planted in the fall, and summer-flowering dahlias, lilies, and gladioli, which are planted in the spring. Most die down after flowering and emerge again the following year, while some are tender and may need overwintering indoors.

SHRUBS Whether they are deciduous or evergreen, these woody-stemmed plants help create a permanent structure. Shrubs range from small thymes and heathers to the treelike *Cotoneaster lacteus* and Portuguese laurel (*Prunus lusitanica*), so check heights and spreads carefully before buying and siting them. Many have pretty flowers and some produce colorful berries and fall foliage.

CLIMBERS These woody-stemmed or perennial plants can be evergreen or deciduous, and most need a support, such as wires or trellis, to scale. Twining types, such as clematis and jasmine, use leaf stalks, tendrils, or stems to coil around a support; the thorny stems of

roses act as hooks to heave themselves up; and self-clinging climbers, including Virginia creeper and ivy, employ adhesive pads or aerial roots.

TREES Whether it is evergreen or deciduous, a tree will provide a sculptural feature and shade. The canopies can be spreading, rounded, conical, or weeping in shape, so check labels and websites to determine the best place for them. Some small trees can also be grown in pots (see *pp.48–53*). Trees may also offer decorative flowers, ornamental bark, and foliage interest.

MARGINALS AND AQUATIC PLANTS
Plants that thrive in water fall into two main categories: marginals, which grow in shallow water, and aquatic plants, including water lilies, which generally grow at depths of 12–36 in (30–90 cm). Some aquatic plants are known as "oxygenators," which are submerged plants that help keep the water clear. For a small space, choose compact species that do not spread quickly (see *pp.116–119*).

Annuals such as pot marigolds (*Calendula officinalis*) live for just a year.

Perennials, including delphiniums, live for three years or more.

Shrubs, for example the guelder rose (*Viburnum opulus*), are long-lived plants.

DESIGNING WITH PLANTS

Plants can transform a dull outdoor space into a haven of foliage and flowers, creating an evolving show of new buds in spring, colorful summer blooms, and fruits in the fall. They can also make a small yard or roof terrace look and feel more spacious by masking the boundaries while increasing your privacy. Plants on a balcony will make it more inviting, creating a beautiful display to enjoy from both inside and out.

Patio roses offer a long season of interest at the front of a raised bed, flowering all summer and into the fall.

Screening boundaries with tall shrubs and trees creates an illusion that the garden extends beyond its limits.

THINK BIG

When designing a tiny space, you may imagine that using small plants tucked next to the boundary walls is the best solution, as it seems to allow more space to move around. However, this simply accentuates the restricted size, allowing all four boundaries to be seen at a glance. In fact, edging your plot with shrubs and small trees that blur the boundaries and including plants in the center of the space to draw your eye away from the sides can make a space look and feel bigger by giving the impression that it extends farther.

PLANT IN LAYERS

Layering your planting, with flowers and foliage growing up to and beyond the height of your boundaries, helps create an illusion of space. To achieve this effect, use a combination of small, medium-size, and tall plants to form a leafy structure that takes your eye from your feet up to the sky. Allow sufficient space for these layers by making the borders at least 3¼ft (1 m) wide, where possible, and try planting perennials and annuals in groups, repeating the same plants throughout the space to create a naturalistic and unified design.

In a smaller area, such as a balcony, use pots to create layers. Place tall plants at the back and small ferns, if your space is shady, or sun-loving succulents such as houseleeks (*Sempervivum*) at the front to create a tapestry of colors and textures. Spring bulbs and summer bedding will add pops of seasonal color.

Using pots of different sizes to create a wall of color, this balcony display includes echeverias and ivy in front and aeoniums at the back.

SEASONAL HIGHLIGHTS

Spring may be the best time to plant your garden, but if you visit a garden center at this time of year and buy the most beautiful plants in bloom you may have nothing to look at when those early flowers start to fade as summer arrives. To create a succession of color and scent, plan your planting to include winter blooms such as mahonias and hellebores, a range of spring bulbs including tulips and daffodils, early- and late-summer flowers, and plants with fall foliage interest, such as a Japanese maple (*Acer palmatum*) or winged spindle (*Euonymus alata*), which both put on a spectacular display.

Combine a collection of tulips with a sweetly scented daphne to brighten up your border in spring.

Fiddle-leaf fig (*Ficus lyrata*), money plant (*Crassula ovata*), and African spear (*Sansevieria cylindrica*) will all be happy outside in summer.

BOOST SUMMER WITH HOUSEPLANTS

You can augment your container plant displays during the summer months by taking a few of your houseplants outside to fill spaces left by spring bulbs or to plug gaps elsewhere. Many leafy houseplants such as the fiddle-leaf fig (*Ficus lyrata*), dwarf umbrella plant (*Schefflera arboricola*), snake plant (*Sansevieria trifasciata*), and succulents will grow well outside, and can add a tropical look to tiny city yards, terraces, or balconies. Just ensure that they are planted in pots with drainage holes in the base and remove their waterproof containers in order to prevent waterlogging. If your houseplants start to look sickly or discolored, they may be too tender for nighttime temperatures in your area and you will need to bring them inside again.

LAWNS AND GROUND COVER

There's nothing like the feel of a lush lawn underfoot in summer, while in winter the fresh green blades provide a splash of color, just when it's wanted most. However, lawns need regular mowing once every week or two during the growing season, so you will require a shed or other storage space to house a mower and other tools to keep your lawn looking pristine.

Lay a lawn in a sunny or lightly shaded area to create a soft green natural carpet for play or relaxing.

SIZING UP

Lawns can be almost any size, but if you want a patch of grass to add impact to a small space, it needs to be large enough to create a design feature and to warrant the effort of taking care of it. The shape of a lawn should be integral to your design scheme and not just a filler for the spaces around beds and borders, which can result in unmanageable strips of grass that look untidy and are difficult to mow. Geometric shapes such as circles, ovals, squares, and rectangles tend to look best, and you can then use the areas around the lawn for paving and planting beds. A hard edge of pavers or bricks around a lawn will help define the shape, too. Install the edging a little lower than the height of the soil surface so you can mow straight over it to create a crisp outline, without the need for edging tools to keep it looking good.

TOP TIP TO REDUCE MOWING MAINTENANCE AND BENEFIT WILDLIFE, LET A LAWN GROW LONGER THAN USUAL. THIS WILL ALLOW BOTH THE GRASS AND FLOWERS IN IT TO BLOOM, PROVIDING FOOD FOR POLLINATORS AND THE CATERPILLARS OF BUTTERFLIES.

Geometric shapes such as squares and circles draw the eye and lend a designer look to a small space.

Laying sod is quick and easy once the ground is prepared, and the grass will be ready to walk on after about four weeks.

LAYING A LAWN

Grass will thrive when it is laid on a free-draining soil surface and maintained with regular mowing and feeding in the spring and fall. Most lawns need a sunny situation that receives about six hours of bright light a day in summer; if your planned site receives less than this, choose a shade-tolerant turf or seed mix. However, remember that lawns rarely grow well in dense shade, such as the area beneath evergreen trees.

The best time to install a lawn is in early fall or mid-spring. A few months beforehand, apply a 2 in (5 cm) organic mulch layer of well-rotted compost or manure over the soil surface, which will improve drainage and add nutrients to feed the grass. When you are ready to lay the lawn, remove all the weeds and, if you have clay soil, apply a layer of washed sharp sand over the soil to improve drainage further and minimize moss growth. Ensure the area is completely level; lumps and bumps will soon look unsightly, as the troughs will collect water run-off from the peaks, resulting in uneven grass growth.

Sow seed evenly (mixing it with fine sand will help you see where you have sown it) or lay sod in a staggered brick-wall pattern. Keep the area well watered and do not walk on your new lawn or mow the grass until it has established and is growing well. This is usually four weeks in the case of turf, or six to eight weeks for seeded lawns.

LOW-MAINTENANCE ALTERNATIVES

There are a few alternatives to lawn grass that require just one cut per year or no mowing at all. Ideal for a small space such as a front yard, these low-growing plants will create an ornamental year-round green carpet, but few will withstand heavy foot traffic. Chamomile is a good choice for a sunny site and only needs a clip annually in late summer; it can be walked on occasionally. Creeping thymes such as *Thymus serpyllum* will tolerate light foot traffic, too, and knit together to form a scented feature. Thyme flowers are loved by bees, so take care not to walk on the lawn when it is in bloom and clip it after flowering. White clover lawns are a popular no-mow option, and will grow in light shade as well as sun. Sow a micro-clover seed mix in spring.

FAKING IT

Artificial grass is a low-maintenance alternative to a natural lawn but it has none of the wildlife benefits. Made from synthetic materials that are nonbiodegradable, it does not provide forage for pollinators nor harbor insects that feed birds, and it can contribute to plastic pollution because it's difficult to recycle and can damage the environment if it ends up in a landfill. These lawns will need cleaning and you may even find weeds take hold in the soil and dirt that builds up between the blades of "grass."

Artificial grass provides an easy-care, durable surface but contributes to plastic pollution.

Chamomile can be used for decorative effect to soften the edges of paving stones in an quiet area that is rarely walked over.

CHOOSING A TREE

Planting a tree in a small space has many benefits, providing height and structure, shade in summer and privacy from neighboring windows, as well as spring flowers, leaf color, and fruits such as apples and pears. A tree also creates a valuable wildlife feature, attracting pollinating insects to the blossoms in spring and birds that use the branches to nest and roost. There are many compact trees suited to small spaces, including tiny ones that can be grown in pots on a patio or terrace.

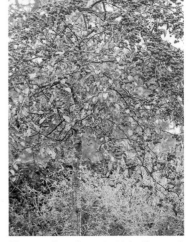

The small crab apple *Malus* 'Evereste' produces a profusion of bright red apples and golden foliage in the fall.

WHY PLANT A TREE?

Many flowering and fruiting trees make colorful focal points in small gardens in spring and fall, while compact conifers offer leaf color all year round. Aside from their aesthetic value, these stately plants also help protect the environment by capturing carbon and storing it in their trunks, roots, and canopies. They do this by absorbing carbon dioxide, one of the gases responsible for global warming, through their leaves and, using light as energy, combining it with water to make glucose in a process known as photosynthesis. All plants make food in this way, but because trees tend to be bigger, they capture relatively larger quantities of carbon, thereby doing the job more effectively than others.

So, by planting a tree in your tiny plot, you will be helping to mitigate the effects of climate change as well as making it more beautiful. Be aware, however, that while more mature trees store larger amounts of carbon than younger saplings, the environmental cost of transporting them may outweigh this benefit.

A gnarled apple tree adds character, as well as blossoms and fruit, to this small flower and edible garden.

SMALL SELECTIONS

Before buying a tree, calculate how much space you have for it and choose a species or cultivar that will not outgrow its welcome a few years after planting. Browse through the recommendations on pp.48–51 and buy from a reputable tree nursery, where the staff will help you select a tree suitable for your plot. Choices include weeping types such as the diminutive *Salix caprea* 'Kilmarnock', which rarely grows to more than 6½ ft (2 m) in height and spread, fruit trees grown on dwarf rootstocks that keep them small, and compact evergreens such as bays and the strawberry tree *Arbutus unedo*, which features white bell-shaped flowers and strawberry-like red fruits.

The willow *Salix caprea* 'Kilmarnock' has a graceful weeping habit and will fit easily into most small spaces.

TREES IN POTS

Small trees grown in pots on a balcony or roof terrace provide many of the benefits offered by trees in yards, but they will require more long-term care. First, check that your structure can take the weight of the pot, potting mix, and plant (see p.82) and then consider how you will keep your little tree watered throughout the year, especially from spring to fall when it is in growth. Lack of water will soon lead to a tree's demise, so make sure someone can help when you are away from home or install an automatic watering system, programming it carefully to ensure it provides the right amount of moisture without flooding your balcony or terrace. Turn to pp.52–53 for a selection of trees suitable for growing in containers.

SITING YOUR TREE

Consider what purpose you want your tree to serve before deciding where to plant it. For example, you may want a tree by a patio or seating area to provide shade in summer, or perhaps you need some privacy from a neighbor's window, in which case you need to think about siting it where the canopy will block their view (see right). Also consider your neighbors' light when planting a tree and check that it will not throw their yard into deep shade. Equally, ensure that the tree does not reduce the light in your own yard—position it on the north side if you want to minimize the shade in your yard, or on the east or west side if you need shade in the morning or evening. Placing it on the south side will cast shadows over the whole yard for many hours each day (see also p.16). Do not plant a tree too close to your property—the width of the root system is usually about equal to the width of the canopy, so a small tree that will grow 10 ft (3 m) wide can be safely planted 12–15 ft (4–5 m) from the house.

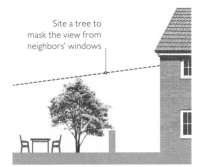

Site a tree to mask the view from neighbors' windows

A well-placed tree can be used both to cast some shade on a seating area and to provide privacy from neighbors.

Compact and slow-growing, Japanese maples are ideal for pots on a balcony or roof terrace.

TOP TIP LEAVE A GAP OF ABOUT 24 IN (60 CM) BETWEEN A TREE AND A WALL OR A FENCE, SINCE THE AREA CLOSE TO THESE STRUCTURES WILL BE IN A RAIN SHADOW AND VERY DRY, HINDERING YOUR TREE'S GROWTH.

HOW TO PLANT A TREE

You can buy either a tree that is sold in the pot in which it has been grown, or a bare-root plant dug up from a field and sold with its root ball wrapped in plastic or burlap. Bare-root trees are generally cheaper, but they are available only from late fall to early spring and should be planted as soon as possible after delivery. Pot-grown trees can be planted at any time of the year, but they will establish more quickly in late fall or early spring, when the seasonal rainfall tends to be higher. Never plant a tree when the soil is waterlogged or frozen, nor during long periods of drought.

A laburnum is a good choice for a small space as long as it isn't used by children or pets, since all parts of this tree are poisonous.

PLANTING TIPS

Follow these simple instructions when planting a pot-grown or bare-root tree to ensure it establishes well.

YOU WILL NEED Bucket • Spade • Fork • Mycorrhizal fungi • Cane • Stake, hammer, and tree tie, if required • Bark chips • Watering can or hose

1 Place your tree's root ball in a bucket of water for about an hour to soak. Meanwhile, dig a square hole three times as wide as the pot or root ball and the same depth. Use a fork to loosen the soil around the sides. Add some mycorrhizal fungi to the bottom of the hole to promote root growth, but do not add any organic matter or compost, which may cause the tree to sink once planted. Place the root ball in the hole and lay a cane across the top to check that the point where the roots meet the stem will be level with, or slightly above, the soil surface once the tree is planted.

2 Remove the tree if it's in a pot and gently loosen the roots if they are coiled around the sides of the root ball. Set the tree in the hole. Refill around it with the excavated soil, checking again that the tree is at the correct level, and press the soil down around the stem with your foot to remove any large air pockets.

3 Water well. Add a stake if your tree needs one (see right), then apply a 2–3-in (5–7.5-cm) layer of bark chips on the soil over the root ball, leaving a 4 in (10 cm) gap around the stem.

4 Newly planted trees must be watered regularly during dry spells for three years after planting. Once or twice a week, water the area using a large can fitted with a fine rose head or a hose on a gentle setting, applying enough water to percolate down to the roots at lower levels. This method mimics a rain shower and will sustain the tree's roots without dislodging the soil.

HIGH STAKES

Large or mature trees and those with a dense leafy canopy and small root ball will need staking. Hammer in a stake at a 45° angle, so that it meets the tree one third of the way up the trunk, with at least 2 ft (60 cm) secured in the ground. Make sure it is leaning into the prevailing wind direction. Attach it using a tree tie, and check every year, loosening the tie as necessary. In two or three years, when the roots are established, remove the stake.

Use a tree tie to secure the stake and loosen annually as the tree grows.

ORNAMENTAL TREES

Choose a small tree that will not outgrow its space or demand regular pruning to keep it neat. Some species are naturally compact, while others have been bred from larger trees to be smaller; take care when buying one of the latter, as there may be a huge difference in size between species and their cultivars, which may be a fraction of the height, as in the case of the Colorado spruce *Picea pungens*. Multi-stemmed trees with three or more trunks growing from one root ball tend to be smaller than those with a single trunk.

SNOWY MESPILUS *AMELANCHIER LAMARCKII*

HEIGHT AND SPREAD up to 26 × 20 ft (8 × 6 m)
SOIL Moist but well-drained
HARDINESS Zones 4–8
SUN ☀ ☀

The deciduous snowy mespilus, or Juneberry, is a favorite among garden designers because it offers many seasons of interest, starting in spring with its white star-shaped flowers that appear as the young bronze leaves emerge. In summer, the foliage matures to dark green, when the edible, purple-black berries, loved by birds, also develop. The show ends in the fall as the tree lights up with fiery red- and orange-tinted leaves. This tree thrives in most soils except very alkaline.

Fiery fall foliage and white spring flowers make this small tree a designer's favorite.

PAPERBARK MAPLE *ACER GRISEUM*

HEIGHT AND SPREAD 26 × 20 ft (8 × 6 m)
SOIL Moist but well-drained
HARDINESS Zones 4–8
SUN ☀ ☀

Prized for its peeling cinnamon-colored bark, this beautiful slow-growing maple has year-round appeal. The deeply cut, lobed leaves provide a cool green leafy canopy in spring and summer before turning brilliant shades of orange and red in the fall. After the foliage has fallen, more of the decorative bark is revealed to create an eye-catching focal point in winter. Remove some lower branches to show off the bark at other times, and select a multi-stemmed tree for maximum impact.

The peeling bark and beautiful foliage of the paperbark maple offer interest year-round.

STRAWBERRY TREE *ARBUTUS UNEDO*

HEIGHT AND SPREAD up to 20 × 20 ft (6 × 6 m)
SOIL Well-drained
HARDINESS Zones 7–10
SUN ☀

If you're looking for year-round color and interest, the strawberry tree more than fits the bill. The peeling red-brown bark and glossy evergreen leaves provide a permanent backdrop to other plantings and, unusually, this tree flowers and fruits at the same time in the fall. The dainty white urn-shaped blooms are often tinged with pink, and appear just as the inedible strawberry-like fruits produced the previous year are turning red. This tree suits a sunny, sheltered urban or coastal garden.

Flowers and fruits appear at the same time in the fall on the evergreen strawberry tree.

CHINESE DOGWOOD *CORNUS KOUSA*

HEIGHT AND SPREAD up to 20 × 12 ft (6 × 4 m)
SOIL Well-drained/moist but well-drained
HARDINESS Zones 5–8
SUN ☼ ☀

There are many named cultivars of this beautiful deciduous tree, which produces small green flowers surrounded by white or pink bracts (petal-like leaves) in summer. The best include 'China Girl', which bears pure white bracts; 'Miss Satomi', with dark pink flower heads; and the species *C. kousa* var. *chinensis*, with white bracts that fade to pink. Strawberry-like fruits follow the blooms, appearing as the leaves turn crimson-purple colors before falling. This tree is best grown in neutral to acid soil.

Cornus kousa var. chinensis produces white summer flowers that age to pink.

HAWTHORN *CRATAEGUS LAEVIGATA*

HEIGHT AND SPREAD 26 × 12 ft (8 × 4 m)
SOIL Well-drained/moist but well-drained
HARDINESS Zones 5–8
SUN ☼ ☀

Hawthorns make excellent trees for small spaces, and *C. laevigata* delivers some of the showiest late-spring blooms. Good choices include 'Rosea Flore Pleno', with its double pink blooms; 'Paul's Scarlet', which produces pinky-red blossoms; and 'Crimson Cloud', with its red and white flowers. The blooms appear after the oak-leaf-like foliage unfurls; this turns buttery-yellow in the fall, when red berries also appear. Bear in mind the tree's thorny stems when looking for a suitable site.

Crataegus laevigata **'Paul's Scarlet'** produces pinky-red flowers in late spring.

CORNELIAN CHERRY *CORNUS MAS*

HEIGHT AND SPREAD 12 × 12 ft (4 × 4 m)
SOIL Well-drained/moist but well-drained
HARDINESS Zones 5–8
SUN ☼ ☀

This large deciduous shrub or small tree is ideal for gardens in need of some color in late winter and early spring, when its clusters of tiny, bright yellow flowers appear on the bare branches. The oval green leaves then unfurl and when the glossy red edible fruits form in the fall, the foliage turns purple before falling. The cultivar 'Aurea' offers yellow-infused green foliage. This little tree is suitable for any small yard or even a large container or raised bed in a courtyard.

Cornelian cherries are among the first trees of the year to bloom.

SOFT TREE FERN *DICKSONIA ANTARCTICA*

HEIGHT AND SPREAD 8 × 8 ft (2.5 × 2.5 m)
SOIL Moist but well-drained
HARDINESS Zones 9–12
SUN ☼ ☀

Creating a focal point in a tropical-themed design, these compact shade-loving trees are a good choice for sheltered town spaces. The leaves form a fountain shape on top of stout reddish-brown trunks to create their distinctive outline. Tree ferns are evergreen in warmer climes, but the foliage will fall during winter in frosty areas, where they will need protection: wrap the stem and crown in layers of horticultural fleece or a cage of straw topped with a waterproof covering.

Tree ferns make an eye-catching statement with their large fronds and stout stems.

STAR MAGNOLIA *MAGNOLIA STELLATA*

HEIGHT AND SPREAD 10 × 12 ft (3 × 4 m)
SOIL Moist but well-drained
HARDINESS Zones 4–8
SUN ☼

Many magnolias are compact trees ideal for small spaces, but the star magnolia is one of the smallest. Its large, star-shaped, white flowers emerge from silky buds in early spring before the mid-green leaves unfurl. While the tree itself is hardy, the blooms, like those of most magnolias, are susceptible to frost damage, so plant it in a sheltered spot out of strong winds that does not receive the morning sun. Aside from that, it is very easy to grow and rarely requires pruning.

The large white flowers of *Magnolia stellata* light up the garden in early spring.

APPLE TREE *MALUS DOMESTICA*

HEIGHT AND SPREAD Up to 12 × 12 ft (4 × 4 m)
SOIL Well-drained/moist but well-drained
HARDINESS Zones 4–9
SUN ☼

The stuff of fairy tales, an apple tree creates a beautiful, feature in a small space, while providing many benefits for wildlife. The white or pink spring blossoms attract bees and other pollinators, and the leafy canopy will provide shade in summer before the fruits form later in the season. Choose from the huge range of apple varieties, and select a tree grafted onto dwarfing rootstock (see p.53). Buy from a reputable nursery that can offer guidance on which tree will suit your site.

Apple trees grafted onto dwarf rootstocks produce an abundant crop in tiny spaces.

CRAB APPLE 'EVEREST' *MALUS* 'EVERESTE'

HEIGHT AND SPREAD Up to 12 × 12 ft (4 × 4 m)
SOIL Well-drained/moist but well-drained
HARDINESS Zones 4–9
SUN ☼

Considered to be one of the best crab apple trees for a small space, 'Evereste' also produces fruits that make delicious jelly. In spring, the stems are covered with red buds that open to reveal white flowers, loved by bees and other pollinators, which appear at the same time as the fresh green leaves emerge. The tree is one of the best for disease resistance and also tolerates pollution. It will grow in most soils but the flowers and fruits need a sunny spot to guarantee a good crop.

Malus **'Evereste'** produces small red fruits in the fall that make a delicious jelly.

PERSIAN IRONWOOD *PARROTIA PERSICA*

HEIGHT AND SPREAD Up to 26 × 26 ft (8 × 8 m)
SOIL Well-drained/moist but well-drained
HARDINESS Zones 5–8
SUN ☼ ☼

This spreading deciduous tree is grown primarily for its spectacular fall color and flaky gray-brown bark, which offers interest in winter. Small, spidery crimson flowers also dress up the yard from late winter, when they appear on bare stems. The green foliage follows in spring, and puts on a dramatic show as it fires up in shades of red, orange, and yellow in late fall or early winter. For tiny spaces, try the cultivar 'Persian Spire', which reaches just 10 ft (3 m) in height and spread.

Persian ironwood's fall colors will light up the yard as the seasons turn.

COLORADO SPRUCE *PICEA PUNGENS* (DWARF CULTIVARS)

HEIGHT AND SPREAD 10 × 6½ ft (3 × 2 m)
SOIL Moist but well-drained; neutral to acidic
HARDINESS Zones 2–8
SUN ☼

Celebrated for its silvery-blue evergreen needles, the dwarf cultivars of the Colorado spruce make excellent trees for a small space. However, check the labels carefully before buying to ensure you don't purchase the species, *Picea pungens*, which is a giant tree, reaching up to 40 ft (12 m) or more. Good dwarf choices include 'Montgomery', with its pyramid of colorful foliage; the very compact 'Edith'; and 'Globosa', which has a more rounded shape. For the best results, grow in soil that leans toward acidic.

Picea pungens 'Montgomery' produces a small, broad pyramid of silvery-blue leaves.

VILMORIN'S ROWAN *SORBUS VILMORINII*

HEIGHT AND SPREAD 15 × 12 ft (5 × 4 m)
SOIL Well-drained/moist but well-drained
HARDINESS Zones 6–8
SUN ☼ ☼

This compact rowan has much to recommend it. The feathery olive-green leaves appear first in spring, followed by flat heads of white flowers, which attract bees and other pollinators. Before dropping in the fall, the foliage turns dark crimson and is accompanied by large eye-catching clusters of red berries that gradually fade to white as the season progresses and last well into winter. The cultivar 'Pink Charm', with its bright pink berries, is a good choice and, like all compact rowans, will suit a small space.

Feathery foliage and red berries that fade to white are this pretty tree's main attractions.

FLOWERING CHERRY *PRUNUS CULTIVARS*

HEIGHT AND SPREAD 12 × 12 ft (4 × 4 m)
SOIL Well-drained/moist but well-drained
HARDINESS Zones 5–9
SUN ☼

If you're looking for spectacular spring blossoms, the small flowering cherries offer it in spades. *Prunus* 'Kursar' is one of the best, with its deep pink single flowers, loved by bees, that open on bare branches. The reddish-bronze foliage then unfurls, maturing to green in summer and turning red and gold before falling. Tolerant of pollution, it also grows well in most soils. Other choices include the pink *P.* 'Accolade'; white-flowered *P. incisa* 'Kojo-no-mai'; and the winter-flowering *P.* × *subhirtella* 'Autumnalis'.

One of the best cherries for a small garden, *Prunus* 'Kursar' produces pink blooms.

IRISH YEW *TAXUS BACCATA* 'FASTIGIATA'

HEIGHT AND SPREAD Up to 26 × 8 ft (8 × 2.5 m)
SOIL Well-drained
HARDINESS Zones 6–8
SUN ☼ ☼ ☀

The elegant, slim shape of this yew creates a visual exclamation mark in a bed or border, its dark evergreen needles offering year-round color. It's easy to trim back if it grows too tall for your liking, but if you do clip it, try to maintain its columnar shape. Mature plants will produce red berries, which are poisonous to humans and pets but loved by birds, who may also nest among its prickly foliage. 'Fastigiata Aurea' has gold-tinted leaves but needs more sun than most for the best color.

The conical outline of a 'Fastigiata' yew creates a year-round focal point.

TREES FOR POTS

The key to growing trees in pots is to provide them with large containers that will allow their roots to expand, and to make sure that their soil never dries out at any point during the year. Containers must also have holes in the base to provide drainage and prevent waterlogging, which can be fatal for many trees. Feed annually in spring with a general-purpose granular fertilizer and repot plants every few years, when you can also trim the roots slightly to keep them compact. The heights and spreads of the trees listed here are the maximum these plants will achieve, and many will remain smaller, their growth restricted by the pot's size.

JAPANESE MAPLE *ACER PALMATUM*

HEIGHT AND SPREAD Up to 8 × 8 ft (2.5 × 2.5 m)
POTTING MIX Peat-free with added topsoil
HARDINESS Zones 5–9
SUN ☼ ☀

Graceful stems of deeply cut foliage, spectacular fall color, and a compact habit make these maples perfect plants for a large container on a patio or balcony. Avoid cultivars with very finely divided leaves, which are prone to drying out and turning brown; opt instead for the purple-leaved cultivar 'Bloodgood'; 'Osakazuki', with its scarlet fall foliage; and the lime-green 'Katsura'. These trees require some sun to put on a colorful show, but also shade for part of the day.

'Bloodgood' produces deep purple lobed foliage that turns bright red in the fall.

AMERICAN REDBUD *CERCIS CANADENSIS* 'FOREST PANSY'

HEIGHT AND SPREAD Up to 12 × 12 ft (4 × 4 m)
POTTING MIX Peat-free with added topsoil
HARDINESS Zones 5–9
SUN ☼ ☀

Displaying large, heart-shaped, red-purple leaves from spring to fall, this multi-stemmed tree makes a dramatic statement in a container on a patio, balcony, or roof terrace. Clusters of small, bright pink flowers appear on the bare stems before the leaves unfurl in spring, and in the fall the foliage turns orange, bronze, and red, ending the year with a spectacular show. In hot summers, move it to an area in part shade to prevent the soil drying, which may result in premature leaf fall.

The American redbud's sparkling fall leaves offer a dramatic finale before dropping.

DWARF FAN PALM *CHAMAEROPS HUMILIS*

HEIGHT AND SPREAD Up to 8 × 5 ft (2.5 × 1.5 m)
POTTING MIX Peat-free with added topsoil
HARDINESS Zones 8–11
SUN ☀

This hardy palm tree will bring a touch of the tropics to your patio or roof terrace, producing a mass of fan-shaped evergreen leaves that create year-round interest. To thrive, the fan palm needs a large container and a warm, slightly shaded position, which will prevent its leaves from scorching, and sharp drainage to ensure the roots don't sit in soggy soil, especially over winter. When siting, allow space around the plant so you can avoid the stems, which are covered with sharp spines.

The dwarf fan palm is one of the hardiest palms, and its fronds put on a show all year.

BAY TREE *LAURUS NOBILIS*

HEIGHT AND SPREAD Up to 12 × 12 ft (4 × 4 m)
POTTING MIX Peat-free with added topsoil
HARDINESS Zones 7–10
SUN ☼ ☼ ☼

Ideal for a formal terrace or kitchen garden, bay can grow into a large tree when unrestrained in the soil but will remain compact if grown in a pot. The glossy, dark, evergreen leaves provide year-round interest and they can be clipped into a shape of your choice. Mature plants may also bear small, pale greenish-yellow flowers and black fruits. Easy to care for, tolerating drought and low light conditions, bay also offers edible leaves—harvest these in spring and summer when the tree is in growth.

Bay trees can be clipped to create graceful, lollipop-shaped heads on single or plaited stems.

DWARF APPLE TREE *MALUS DOMESTICA*

HEIGHT AND SPREAD Up to 8 × 6½ ft (2.5 × 2 m)
POTTING MIX Peat-free with added topsoil
HARDINESS Zones 4–9
SUN ☼

There are many apple trees bred for growing in pots, and a good nursery will offer a selection grafted on either extreme dwarfing (M27) or dwarfing (M9) rootstocks that will thrive in a container. You will need to grow two trees if you select a variety that requires a pollination partner to produce fruit, so check with your supplier before buying. As well as the sweet fruits in the fall, you can also enjoy the pollen-rich blossoms in spring, which will attract bees. See also p.50 for more small fruit trees.

Fruiting trees on extreme dwarfing rootstocks are suitable for containers on a balcony.

DWARF MOUNTAIN PINE *PINUS MUGO*

HEIGHT AND SPREAD Up to 8 × 12 ft (2.5 × 4 m)
POTTING MIX Peat-free with added topsoil
HARDINESS Zones 3–7
SUN ☼

This dwarf pine makes a beautiful specimen tree for a container, its short, dark green needles delivering year-round color and the dark brown cones offering further interest when they appear in the fall. Make sure your pot has good drainage but keep the soil consistently moist during the growing season from spring to early fall. There are many cultivars available, including the popular 'Mops' which reaches about 3¼ ft (1 m) in height and spread, and 'Winter Gold', with its green foliage, tinted gold in winter.

Pinus mugo **'Mops'** creates a beautiful rounded canopy of dark green needles.

CHERRY 'THE BRIDE' *PRUNUS* 'THE BRIDE'

HEIGHT AND SPREAD Up to 8 × 6½ ft (2.5 × 2 m) in a pot
POTTING MIX Peat-free with added topsoil
HARDINESS Zones 5–8
SUN ☼

If you have a sunny, sheltered patio or roof terrace, this small ornamental cherry tree will make a beautiful focal point. This is particularly the case in early spring, when the bare branches are decked with dainty white flowers that resemble a bride's veil. The green foliage adds a cool note in summer before taking on its fall guise, when the leaves turn red and orange before falling. It is ideal for a large container; keep it well watered to guarantee a good annual show and prune wayward stems in summer.

Prunus **'The Bride'** creates a spectacular show when the white spring blossoms appear.

BEAUTIFUL BORDERS

You can create a bed or border almost anywhere, in sun or shade, if you choose plants adapted to the conditions (see pp.58–67). Avoid planting in areas close to walls, fences, and hedges, which will be very dry, or make your border wide enough to plant 18 in (45 cm) away from these structures, where there will be more moisture. Take time to improve the soil before planting and plan your arrangements carefully to include plants that perform at different times of the year to create a beautiful, evolving picture you can enjoy throughout the seasons.

Create long-term interest with a leafy Japanese maple, grasses, and late summer-flowering sedums, which also look beautiful in bud, as seen here.

BIG IS BEST

While space in small gardens is limited, if you want to layer your planting for year-round interest (see pp.40–41), try to make your beds and borders at least 3¼ft (1 m) wide and as long as possible. If they are too narrow, you will be able to fit in only one layer of planting, which may limit the interest to just a season or two, when it is in bloom. Another

disadvantage is that the plant stems may sprawl untidily beyond their boundaries onto grass or a path.

Beds can be any shape; you can fit them around a lawn (see pp.42–43), patio, or path, or use them to make a statement in their own right. Whichever design you choose, avoid fussy shapes and wiggly lines, opting instead for broad, sweeping curves or simple squares and rectangles for a clean, impactful design.

Mulching beds annually with rotted compost or manure will improve the soil structure, allowing plants to thrive.

A BETTER BED

To make a new bed, follow the instructions on pp.56–57, and improve the soil by laying an organic mulch over the surface either before or after planting and every year thereafter (see p.17). Also add mulches to existing beds to improve their performance. Source soil conditioner, well-rotted homemade compost, or manure from an organic farm or stable and spread a 2 in (5 cm) layer around the plants, keeping it clear of shrub and tree stems. As well as improving the soil structure, a mulch will protect it from erosion and reduce weed growth. It will trap moisture beneath it, too, keeping roots hydrated and reducing plants' irrigation needs.

Deep beds allow space for a range of plants that can provide year-round interest with their leaves, stems, and flowers.

WHEN TO PLANT

You can plant pot-grown plants at any time of year, but they are more likely to establish well in early fall or mid-spring, when the soil is warm and moist. If you are planning to include drought-loving plants, such as lavender, rock roses (*Cistus*), and Russian sage (*Salvia*), wait until spring, which will give them a few seasons to establish before winter, increasing their survival rate. Never plant when the soil is frozen or waterlogged, nor in summer, unless you are able to water new plants regularly.

Add tender summer annuals after the frosts in late spring to fill gaps between the more permanent plants in a border.

Stone chips form a boundary between a bed and the lawn.

EDGING OPTIONS

Creating a hard edge to flank your bed or border helps define its shape, and if it's next to a lawn, a paved or gravel surface will prevent plants from trailing over the grass and killing it. Upright edging made from clay tiles, or timber, steel, or recycled materials will create a neat boundary around a bed, though it may not prevent plants from flopping over a lawn. You can also use these border edgings to create shallow raised beds.

Timber edging can be used to create a raised bed.

MIXED PLANS

In a small space, using a combination of evergreen and deciduous shrubs, flowering perennials, seasonal bulbs, and annuals to fill any gaps will deliver a year-round display. Follow the advice on layering plants and including seasonal highlights on pp.40–41, and check plant labels to ensure you site them where they will receive the light they require.

Leave sufficient space between your plants to allow them to grow to their full potential. This is particularly important when positioning trees, shrubs, and large plants that may be more difficult to move once established. Perennials and bulbs can be planted closer together for instant impact because most are easy to divide and move if they outgrow their space.

Alliums, salvias, nepeta, and artemisia combine to provide a long season of color in this sunny border.

MAKING A FLOWERBED

Making a new flowerbed in your garden is easy, though planning ahead to ensure the soil is well prepared will help get your plants off to a good start. Begin by creating a bed in early fall or early spring, clearing the space of any large stones or rubble and removing all weeds. Hoe off annuals and dig out the roots of pernicious ones such as dandelions and brambles (*see pp.130–131*) to give your new plants the best start.

YOU WILL NEED Tape measure • Hose or peg and string • Sand or landscaping paint • Sod cutter • Spade • Fork • Well-rotted compost or manure • Plants of your choice • Mycorrhizal fungi

1 Measure out your bed, using a hose to create a smooth curve or a peg and string to make a circle. Mark the shape with sand or landscaping paint. Remove any weeds and grass, which you can compost.

2 Fork over the surface to loosen compacted soil. Leave the bed for a few weeks, then remove any new weeds that have appeared. Set out your planting on the bed, placing trees and large shrubs first, then filling the gaps between them with perennials, grasses, bulbs, and annuals. Check that the plants will receive the sun and space they need.

3 Water the plants. To plant a tree, see pp.46–47. For all other plants, dig a hole for each one, about the same depth and 2–3 times as wide as the root ball. Fork the bottom of the hole to remove any compaction, and add some mycorrhizal fungi to the base, which encourages strong root growth.

4 Place the plant in the hole, making sure that it will be at the same depth in the ground as it was in its pot. Backfill with soil and firm down to remove large air pockets. Water well and add an organic mulch (*see p.17*) if you haven't already done so. Irrigate until all the plants are well established.

Create a riot of color using perennials such as pinks, geraniums, aquilegias, and foxgloves.

PLANTS FOR A FLOWERBED

Once you have organized your planting spaces, browse the plants for a sunny bed on the next few pages and turn to pp.64–67 for a range of shade-lovers. Look through the plant directories elsewhere in the book, too, for other suggestions that may suit your space. Combine shrubs for structure and bulbs and perennials to introduce seasonal color, checking plants' sizes to ensure they will fit. Perennials and bulbs often achieve their full height and spread within a couple of years, while shrubs may take many years to achieve their full potential.

GLOSSY ABELIA *ABELIA × GRANDIFLORA*

HEIGHT AND SPREAD up to 8 × 8 ft (2.5 × 2.5 m)
SOIL Moist but well-drained
HARDINESS Zones 6–9
SUN ☼

Semi-evergreen and fairly slow-growing, this shrub produces arching stems of small, glossy leaves and pale pink, slightly fragrant flowers from midsummer to fall. It needs sun to produce the best displays of bell-shaped blooms and will survive periods of drought once established. 'Edward Goucher' is a compact form with lilac-pink flowers, while the variegated 'Kaleidoscope' has yellow and green foliage that takes on orange and red tints in the fall. Remove old stems after flowering.

'Edward Goucher' is a compact abelia, reaching just 5 ft (1.5 m) when mature.

ORNAMENTAL ONION *ALLIUM*

HEIGHT AND SPREAD up to 39 × 8 in (100 × 20 cm)
SOIL Well-drained
HARDINESS Zones 3–8
SUN ☼ ☼

Perfect for filling gaps in a late spring border, *Allium hollandicum* creates a striking display of pompom flower heads in shades of purple or white, held aloft on slim stems. 'Purple Sensation' is the most popular, with its deep violet spherical blooms. A shorter, equally beautiful form is *Allium neapolitanum* Cowanii Group, the curved stems of which look like swans' necks before they lift up to reveal clusters of white, star-shaped flowers. The leaves may die down as the flowers open. Plant allium bulbs in the fall.

'Purple Sensation' features tall, slim stems topped with deep violet flower heads.

CALIFORNIAN LILAC *CEANOTHUS*

HEIGHT AND SPREAD up to 10 × 10 ft (3 × 3 m)
SOIL Well-drained
HARDINESS Zones 8–10
SUN ☼

Californian lilacs are evergreen shrubs that burst into bloom in late spring or from late summer to fall, when their oval heads of blue, white, or pink flowers open. Some make large shrubs while others are more compact, so choose one that suits your space. You can train *Ceanothus thyrsiflorus* var. *repens*, C. 'Concha', and others with lax stems onto wires to cover a wall or fence. These shrubs are not fully hardy, so give them a sheltered spot in full sun. Prune after flowering, or in spring in the case of fall-flowering shrubs.

Ceanothus thyrsiflorus* var. *repens can be trained on wires to cover a wall or fence.

RED VALERIAN *CENTRANTHUS RUBER*

HEIGHT AND SPREAD 32 × 18 in (80 × 45 cm)
SOIL Well-drained, neutral to alkaline
HARDINESS Zones 5–8
SUN ☼ ☼

If you need a stalwart for a sunny border that will flower continuously from summer to fall, red valerian is ideal. This tough perennial produces blue-green, spear-shaped leaves and clusters of tiny pinkish-red flowers that are loved by bees; the cultivar 'Albus' has white flowers. Once established, it will rarely, if ever, need watering and may self-seed to other areas of the garden—simply pull out any unwanted seedlings. It also tolerates salt-laden air close to the coast.

Red valerian produces its reddish-pink flower heads from summer to fall.

MONTBRETIA *CROCOSMIA*

HEIGHT AND SPREAD up to 3¼ × 3¼ ft (1 × 1 m)
SOIL Well-drained
HARDINESS Zones 5–9
SUN ☼ ☼

Brightening up the summer garden with their arching stems of dazzling red, orange, or yellow blooms, montbretia are easy-to-grow, trouble-free plants for sunny, sheltered gardens. Their strappy mid-green foliage also provides interest earlier in the year. Plant them en masse in spring for maximum effect, and leave the foliage to die down naturally after flowering in the fall. Restrain tall varieties such as 'Lucifer' with stakes if they are flopping over their neighbors. Lift and divide large clumps in spring.

'George Davison' produces spikes of amber-yellow flowers and sword-shaped leaves.

JAPANESE SNOW FLOWER *DEUTZIA GRACILIS*

HEIGHT AND SPREAD up to 3¼ × 3¼ ft (1 × 1 m)
SOIL Moist but well-drained
HARDINESS Zones 4–8
SUN ☼ ☼

The bright green leaves of this compact deciduous shrub provide an attractive backdrop for its sprays of clear white star-shaped flowers, which produce a sweet perfume when they open from late spring to early summer. Where space is tight, choose 'Nikko', a dwarf form that rarely exceeds 2 ft (60 cm) in height and spread. This shrub requires little care after it has established, but pruning the stem tips in summer after it has flowered will encourage a bushier habit and more blooms.

The Japanese snow flower's scented blooms will perfume the air in a small garden during late spring.

GLOBE THISTLE *ECHINOPS*

HEIGHT AND SPREAD up to 6 × 2 ft (1.8 × 0.6 m)
SOIL Well-drained
HARDINESS Zones 3–8
SUN ☼ ☼

The spiny, lobed, gray-green leaves of the globe thistle are joined in summer by long-lasting globe-shaped blue flower heads that are loved by butterflies and bees. Some of these handsome perennials are large and need adequate space to perform well, so check labels carefully for a cultivar that suits your space. *Echinops bannaticus* 'Taplow Blue' will help fill the back of a sunny border, or try the shorter *E. ritro* 'Veitch's Blue' for the middle of a bed. The fall seed heads are also loved by birds.

The spiny foliage and round purple flowers of 'Veitch's Blue' create a striking focal point.

SEA HOLLY *ERYNGIUM*

HEIGHT AND SPREAD up to 36 × 24 in (90 × 60 cm)
SOIL Well-drained
HARDINESS Zones 3–8
SUN ☼

Loved for their spiny foliage, eye-catching blue stems, and thistlelike flower heads, this group of perennials will thrive in a sunny position and very free-draining soil. Popular species include *E. bourgatii*, with its marbled foliage and silvery-blue flower heads, which grows to 18 in (45 cm); *E. × zabelii* 'Jos Eijking', which produces silver cones surrounded by bright blue spiny ruffs; and the tall, silvery *E. giganteum*, a short-lived perennial that can be grown from seed in spring. All sea hollies are loved by bees.

E. amethystinum has steely-blue spiky flower heads surrounded by silvery bracts.

AVENS *GEUM*

HEIGHT AND SPREAD 24 × 24 in (60 × 60 cm)
SOIL Well-drained/moist but well-drained
HARDINESS Zones 3–7
SUN ☼ ☼

With an exceptionally long flowering season, avens are a must for the front of a bed or border, where their green, frilly-edged leaves will form a skirt beneath wiry stems topped with little round blooms. The flowers come in a range of shades, from bright red to tangerine-orange and yellow—some of them bicolored—and appear for most of the summer. These perennials need little aftercare once established, although mulching around plants in spring will help keep them thriving.

Avens' colorful flowers will brighten up the front of a bed when they appear in summer.

ROCK ROSE *HELIANTHEMUM*

HEIGHT AND SPREAD 12 × 24 in (30 × 60 cm)
SOIL Well-drained, neutral to alkaline
HARDINESS Zones 5–10
SUN ☼ ☼

The spreading stems of this evergreen shrub create a graceful cascading effect when left to trail over the sides of a raised bed or garden wall, or form a carpet over the soil at the front of a sunny border. The tiny gray-green leaves are covered with white, yellow, or pink round flowers for many weeks from mid-spring to midsummer, offering a long season of color. When established, this trouble-free shrub needs almost no aftercare, apart from pruning back overly long stems in mid- or late summer.

Pastel-pink flowers stand out against the gray-green foliage of 'Rhodanthe Carneum'.

DAYLILY *HEMEROCALLIS*

HEIGHT AND SPREAD up to 3¼ × 4 ft (1 × 1.2 m)
SOIL Moist but well-drained
HARDINESS Zones 4–9
SUN ☼ ☼

Fountains of green strappy leaves are followed in summer by trumpet-shaped blooms that each last just one day, giving rise to this perennial's common name. However, the flowers are produced in succession, resulting in a long season of interest. The huge choice of daylilies includes tall and shorter plants and flowers in almost every color except blue and purple. Be prepared to deadhead the faded blooms regularly to keep the plant looking neat, and cut flowering stems down to the ground when blooming is finished.

'Sammy Russell' is an eye-catching daylily with dark red and orange-yellow flowers.

BEARDED IRIS *IRIS*

HEIGHT AND SPREAD up to 4 × 2 ft (1.2 × 0.6 m)
SOIL Well-drained
HARDINESS Zones 3–10
SUN ☀

Irises are named after the Greek word for rainbow, which reflects the species' broad spectrum of flower colors. Bearded irises display soft filaments on their drooping petals, known as "falls," giving rise to their common name. Sword-shaped leaves appear in spring, followed by tall stems of colorful flowers that often comprise a few different hues. Plant the rhizomes so that the top half is above the soil surface, exposed to the sun, and reduce the leaves by a third of their length.

Tall and elegant, the flowers of bearded irises often include petals of different hues.

RED HOT POKER *KNIPHOFIA*

HEIGHT AND SPREAD up to 4 × 2 ft (1.2 × 0.6 m)
SOIL Moist but well-drained
HARDINESS Zones 5–9
SUN ☀ ◑

For a stand-out plant you can't ignore, the red hot poker comes top of the list. The strappy foliage plays second fiddle to the tall stems of torch-like flower heads, which usually appear in late summer, although some flower earlier. The blooms come in shades of red, yellow, and orange, while some, including *Kniphofia uvaria*, sport bicolored yellow and red flowers that look as if the tips are on fire. Dwarf cultivars are also available. These easy-care perennials will bloom year after year.

'Buttercup' features bright yellow flowers that gradually open from green buds.

DWARF CATMINT *NEPETA RACEMOSA*

HEIGHT AND SPREAD 24 × 24 in (60 × 60 cm)
SOIL Moist but well-drained
HARDINESS Zones 4–8
SUN ☀ ◑

A member of the mint family, this perennial has aromatic gray-green leaves that attract cats, who love to roll in it. Aside from pleasing pets, *Nepeta* is grown for its bright lavender-blue summer flowers that make a decorative frill at the front of a border and bloom for many weeks. You can also clip them back after the first flush to encourage an even longer flowering period. Catmint tolerates a wide range of conditions, including wet winters and dry summers. 'Walker's Low' is a popular compact variety.

Catmint creates a mound of lilac-blue flowers, loved by bees, for a long period in summer.

GAURA *OENOTHERA LINDHEIMERI*

HEIGHT AND SPREAD up to 5 × 3 ft (1.5 × 0.9 m)
SOIL Moist but well-drained
HARDINESS Zones 5–9
SUN ☀ ◑

Previously known as *Gaura lindheimeri*, these elegant plants produce small green leaves below tall wands covered with dainty flowers that look like little butterflies as they dance in the breeze. The pink or white blooms of these perennials appear over a long period from summer to early fall and are loved by bees. Plant gaura in a sheltered sunny or lightly shaded spot where strong winds won't damage the stems. The Geyser series is more compact than the species but not quite as hardy.

More compact than the species, the Geyser series is ideal for the middle of a bed.

RUSSIAN SAGE *SALVIA YANGII*

HEIGHT AND SPREAD up to 4 × 3¼ft (1.2 × 1 m)
SOIL Well-drained
HARDINESS Zones 4–9
SUN ☼

The slim, aromatic gray-green leaves of Russian sage, formerly known as *Perovskia atriplicifolia*, are held on white stems and provide a textured backdrop for early-summer blooms. Violet-blue flowers then appear above the leaves later in the season. This deciduous sub-shrub is best planted in full sun at the back of a border; choose 'Little Spire', which reaches about 2 ft (60 cm) in height, for the front or middle of a bed. It is easy to grow—simply prune all the stems down to about 12 in (30 cm) in spring.

'Blue Spire' produces tall stems of bright violet-blue flowers from late summer.

BLACK-EYED SUSAN *RUDBECKIA FULGIDA*

HEIGHT AND SPREAD 32 × 24 in (80 × 60 cm)
SOIL Moist but well-drained
HARDINESS Zones 5–9
SUN ☼ ☼

After early summer-flowering plants have faded, the bold blooms of black-eyed susans burst on to the scene with an explosion of color. These sturdy perennials produce small lance-shaped leaves and masses of cone-shaped golden daisies with dark brown centers from late summer to early fall. *R. fulgida* var. *sullivantii* 'Goldsturm' is a compact variety with a long flowering season. While these plants will cope with a little shade, they may need staking in these situations as the stems reach for the light.

Dark-centered yellow daisies bring a sense of drama to borders from late summer.

BALKAN CLARY *SALVIA NEMOROSA*

HEIGHT AND SPREAD up to 24 × 24 in (60 × 60 cm)
SOIL Moist but well-drained
HARDINESS Zones 3–8
SUN ☼

As you would expect from a sage, the Balkan clary produces stems of aromatic gray-green textured foliage, which go almost unnoticed in a border until the slender spires of violet-blue flowers appear in midsummer. You can extend the flowering period into the fall by removing the spikes as soon as the flowers start to fade. Loved by bees, the blooms provide a vertical accent at the front or in the middle of a border; while plants will cope with a little light shade, they perform best in full sun.

'Ostfriesland' is a compact form of Balkan clary with violet-blue late-summer flowers.

MOOR GRASS *SESLERIA AUTUMNALIS*

HEIGHT AND SPREAD up to 24 × 24 in (60 × 60 cm)
SOIL Well-drained/moist but well-drained
HARDINESS Zones 5–9
SUN ☼ ☼

Offering cool relief to the brighter flowers in a border, evergreen moor grass is loved by garden designers for its clumps of arching gray-green foliage, which take on brighter lime-green tints in the fall. During the summer months, the leaves are joined by wands of flowers, the silky blooms resembling white candles when they catch the sun. This easy-to-grow grass is also happy in part shade, and tolerates most soils, apart from wet. Cut back old foliage in spring.

Moor grass produces hummocks of gently arching leaves that provide a cool green contrast to seasonal flowers.

MICHAELMAS DAISY *SYMPHYOTRICHUM*

HEIGHT AND SPREAD up to 36 × 18 in (90 × 45 cm)
SOIL Moist but well-drained
HARDINESS Zones 3–8
SUN ☼ ☼

Michaelmas daisies, or asters, create dazzling displays of blue, purple, pink, or white flowers from late summer to mid-fall. These perennials come in a range of sizes from mid-border stalwarts to compact dwarf plants. Popular cultivars include the tall 'Little Carlow', which has small, violet-blue late-summer flowers; the compact New York aster *S. novae-angliae* 'Purple Dome', with its bright purple blooms; and *S. ericoides* 'Pink Cloud', which produces tiny pale pink flowers. Tall varieties may need staking.

'Little Carlow' is a popular cultivar with tall stems of yellow-eyed violet daisies.

TULIP *TULIPA*

HEIGHT AND SPREAD up to 24 × 8 in (60 × 20 cm)
SOIL Well-drained
HARDINESS Zones 3–7
SUN ☼ ☼

No spring garden is complete without a few tulips. Choose from the vast array of flower colors and shapes, and plant the bulbs in groups for the most dramatic effects. Darwin hybrids are the tallest types, while the tiny species tulips (see p.87) will decorate the front of a border. If you have space, include a few selections that bloom at different times to prolong your display. Species tulips will reappear year after year after an initial planting but many others won't, so plant fresh bulbs each fall.

The orange-red blooms of 'Prinses Irene' create a striking contrast with forget-me-nots.

PURPLE TOP *VERBENA BONARIENSIS*

HEIGHT AND SPREAD up to 4 × 2 ft (1.2 × 0.6 m)
SOIL Well-drained
HARDINESS Zones 7–11
SUN ☼

You can squeeze the tall, slim, square-shaped stems of purple top between other plants in a border, making this elegant perennial one of the best for a small space. The clusters of small purple flowers, which have a faint clove scent and are loved by bees and butterflies, add spots of color at eye-level when they appear from summer to early fall. Very easy to grow if you have free-draining soil and a sunny, sheltered site, purple top may also self-seed into areas that suit it, particularly in gravel.

The see-through stems of purple top create the effect of a semitransparent veil of color.

WEIGELA *WEIGELA*

HEIGHT AND SPREAD up to 6½ × 6½ ft (2 × 2 m)
SOIL Well-drained/moist but well-drained
HARDINESS Zones 4–8
SUN ☼ ☼

Weigelas are easy-to-grow deciduous shrubs, loved for their long flowering season and the wide choice of colors and sizes. Their trumpet-shaped, pollen-rich blooms appear from late spring to summer and come in shades of pink, red, purple, yellow, and white. There is also a choice of foliage colors, including bronze, purple, and variegated forms. While some weigelas are the size of a small tree, others, such as 'Ebony and Ivory' and 'Picobella Rosa', will just reach your knees. Prune after flowering.

'Eva Rathke' is a compact form of weigela with dark pink trumpet-shaped blooms.

JAPANESE ANEMONE *ANEMONE X HYBRIDA*

HEIGHT AND SPREAD up to 5 x 4 ft (1.5 x 1.2 m)
SOIL Moist but well-drained
HARDINESS Zones 4–8
SUN ☼ ☼

Ideal for the back of a border in a semi-shaded spot, Japanese anemones bring the late summer and early fall garden to life with their tall stems of white or pink flowers. The blooms attract bees and other pollinators and appear above maplelike lobed foliage. This perennial is quick to spread, forming large clumps after a few years, which can be a blessing or a curse, depending on your view. *A. x hybrida* is less invasive than *A. hupehensis*, so check labels carefully since they look almost identical.

The elegant white flowers of 'Honorine Jobert' will brighten up a gloomy area.

MASTERWORT *ASTRANTIA*

HEIGHT AND SPREAD 24 x 24 in (60 x 60 cm)
SOIL Moist but free-draining
HARDINESS Zones 4–9
SUN ☼ ☼

Loved by florists for their unusual flowers, which comprise a pincushion of stamens surrounded by a ruff of slim petals, these compact perennials are a must for a small, partly shaded space. The blooms come in shades of pink, red, cream, and white, and are held on wiry stems above lobed foliage. They are easy to grow and tolerate a wide range of soils, although they grow best in moisture-retentive loams. Help the soil stay hydrated by applying an organic mulch *(see p.17)* around the plants each year.

'Roma' is a clear pink cultivar that flowers in early summer and often again in the fall.

ELEPHANT'S EARS *BERGENIA*

HEIGHT AND SPREAD up to 24 x 30 in (60 x 75 cm)
SOIL Well-drained/moist but well-drained
HARDINESS Zones 5–8
SUN ☼ ☼

An evergreen perennial, elephant's ears produces large, glossy, round leaves, and clusters of bell-shaped pink or white flowers in spring. *Bergenia purpurascens* and *B. cordifolia* 'Purpurea' provide further interest in winter, when their foliage takes on red or purple tints. Easy-to-grow and fairly drought-tolerant once established, bergenias need little aftercare: in spring, remove old or tatty foliage, and lift and divide congested plants. Also remove faded flower stems to keep the plants tidy.

The large glossy leaves and pink spring flowers of *Bergenia cordifolia* provide all-year color.

BUTTERFLY BUSH *BUDDLEIA DAVIDII*

HEIGHT AND SPREAD up to 10 x 10 ft (3 x 3 m)
SOIL Well-drained/moist but well-drained
HARDINESS Zones 5–10
SUN ☼ ☼

Prized for their large, cone-shaped, scented flower heads, which are loved by butterflies, these deciduous shrubs are tolerant of most soils and shade. The summer blooms come in a range of colors, including purple, blue, red, pink, and yellow. Use them to add color to the back of a border, or select a dwarf *Buddleia* such as one of the Chip Series for the front to middle of a bed. Pruning large varieties back hard in spring will keep them compact and encourage more flowers to form.

Buddleia features large, cone-shaped, nectar-rich flower heads in summer that attract butterflies and bees.

BUTTERCUP WITCH HAZEL *CORYLOPSIS PAUCIFLORA*

HEIGHT AND SPREAD 5 × 8 ft (1.5 × 2.5 m)
SOIL Well-drained/moist but well-drained
HARDINESS Zones 6–9
SUN ☼

This slow-growing deciduous shrub has much to offer, brightening up the spring garden with its drooping clusters of pale yellow, sweetly scented flowers, which appear on bare stems, and oval leaves that are tinged red when young. The bright green mature foliage then makes a backdrop for other colorful flowers in summer. Plant *Corylopsis* close to a path or where you can appreciate the spring perfume. It will grow well in most soils, and thrives in a shady border. Prune in late spring or early summer after flowering.

The highly scented flowers of the buttercup witch hazel perfume the air in early spring.

FOXGLOVE *DIGITALIS PURPUREA*

HEIGHT AND SPREAD up to 5ft × 20in (1.5 × 0.5m)
SOIL Well-drained/moist but well-drained
HARDINESS Zones 4–9
SUN ☼ ☼

No shade garden is complete without a few foxgloves. These biennials or short-lived perennials produce large, soft, oval leaves beneath tall spikes of tubular flowers, speckled within to lure bees to their stores of nectar. Choose blooms in shades of pink, purple, apricot, orange, or white, or select a bicolored cultivar. When happy, foxgloves will self-seed, but you may have to sow or buy young plants each year to guarantee a summer display. If sowing seed, remember that biennials only bloom in the second year.

Foxgloves add tall accents to a partly shaded border with their spikes of tubular flowers.

MALE FERN *DRYOPTERIS*

HEIGHT AND SPREAD up to 3¼ × 3¼ft (1 × 1 m)
SOIL Well-drained/moist but well-drained
HARDINESS Zones 5–9
SUN ☼ ☼

Ideal for the darkest corners, the male fern produces large, handsome fronds of bright green divided leaves for most of the year. *Dryopteris filix-mas* tolerates the dry soil conditions beneath trees, while *D. affinis* needs a little more moisture. For a splash of spring color, also try the deciduous autumn fern, *D. erythrosora*, which has coppery-red young leaves that mature to dark green. In spring, remove the old fronds to make way for new growth and mulch the soil around your ferns to lock in moisture.

Dryopteris affinis bears bright green, semi-evergreen fronds that may last through winter.

BARRENWORT *EPIMEDIUM*

HEIGHT AND SPREAD 16 × 24in (40 × 60cm)
SOIL Moist but well-drained
HARDINESS Zones 3–9
SUN ☼ ☼

The heart-shaped leaves of this evergreen or semi-evergreen perennial create a carpet of color and texture beneath trees and shrubs. In spring, dainty nodding flowers in shades of yellow, orange, or pink also appear. Choices include *E.* × *perralchicum* with its yellow flowers and bronze-tinted foliage in spring and fall; *E.* × *rubrum*, which has red-tinted foliage and red and yellow blooms; and *E.* × *cantabrigiense*, with coppery-pink flowers above colorful leaves. Remove the old foliage in early spring..

The copper-tinted young foliage of *Epimedium perralchicum* creates a colorful carpet.

SPURGE *EUPHORBIA*

HEIGHT AND SPREAD 2 × 3¼ ft (0.6 × 1 m)
SOIL Well-drained/moist but well-drained
HARDINESS Zones 4–8
SUN ☼ ☀

A few spurges are adapted to life in the shade, including *Euphorbia amygdaloides* var. *robbiae*, which also copes with dry soils. This tough evergreen perennial forms rosettes of slim, dark green leaves and upright stems topped with small yellow-green flowers from late spring to summer. Alternatively, try the deciduous *E. griffithii*, with dark green leaves edged red to match the early summer blooms. Cut back the faded flowering stems, wearing gloves to protect your hands from the toxic sap.

Euphorbia amygdaloides* var. *robbiae copes with dry shade beneath trees and shrubs.

HELLEBORE *HELLEBORUS*

HEIGHT AND SPREAD up to 18 × 18 in (45 × 45 cm)
SOIL Well-drained
HARDINESS Zones 6–9
SUN ☼ ☀

Flowering from late winter to mid-spring, hellebores' round, nodding blooms come in shades of green, white, purple, pink, or red. These evergreen perennials also produce decorative leathery leaves, which feature marbling patterns in some plants. The Christmas rose, *Helleborus niger*, is one of the first to bloom, from midwinter, while the popular Oriental hybrids (*H. × hybridus*) flower a little later. A few, including *H. sternii*, are not fully hardy. Remove old and tatty foliage before the flowers open.

The pink-tinted white flowers of *Helleborus* × *ericsmithii* appear above mottled foliage in spring.

ROCK CRANESBILL *GERANIUM MACRORRHIZUM*

HEIGHT AND SPREAD 18 × 24 in (45 × 60 cm)
SOIL Well-drained/moist
HARDINESS Zones 4–8
SUN ☼ ☀

One of the best cranesbills for shade, this semi-evergreen perennial produces a textured mat of soft, apple-green, scented foliage, which in late spring or early summer is joined by dainty little flowers that last for many weeks. The color range includes blooms in shades of pink, purple, or white. Useful as a weed suppressant under trees and shrubs, this pretty plant copes with dry shade and may self-seed into other areas. Remove old and tatty foliage in spring before the flowers appear.

In early summer, 'Czakor' produces bright magenta blooms that shine out of the shade.

CORAL BELLS *HEUCHERA*

HEIGHT AND SPREAD 20 × 20 in (50 × 50 cm)
SOIL Well-drained/moist but well-drained
HARDINESS Zones 4–9
SUN ☼ ☀

Grown for their colorful foliage, coral bells produce mounds of lobed evergreen leaves in colors ranging from burgundy, purple, and pink to silver and orange, as well as every shade of green you can imagine. In summer, tiny pink or white flowers appear on wiry stems above the foliage. These perennials create a weed-suppressing mat in partially shaded areas, and they are also useful in container displays. Remove old and tatty foliage in spring, and mulch around plants at the same time.

'Palace Purple' bears dark burgundy leaves and tiny pink summer flowers on wiry stems.

BLEEDING HEART *LAMPROCAPNOS SPECTABILIS*

HEIGHT AND SPREAD up to 3¼ × 3¼ ft (1 × 1 m)
SOIL Moist but well-drained
HARDINESS Zones 3–9
SUN ☀

Elegant, arching stems dripping with pendent heart-shaped pink and white flowers create a focal point when they appear in late spring over fernlike green foliage. Choose the cultivar 'Alba' if you prefer pure white blooms. The flowers last for a few weeks; after they have faded the whole plant dies down, leaving little trace by midsummer, so plant it where others will disguise the gap and ensure you don't dig it up when dormant. Easy to grow, it needs no extra care once established.

'Alba' produces elegant, pure white heart-shaped flowers on arching stems in spring.

BORDER PHLOX *PHLOX PANICULATA*

HEIGHT AND SPREAD up to 3¼ × 3¼ ft (1 × 1 m)
SOIL Moist but free-draining
HARDINESS Zones 4–8
SUN ☀ ☀

Most phlox, including the ground-hugging *Phlox subulata* and this taller border plant, will grow happily in some shade. The dark green lance-shaped leaves of the border phlox appear in spring and are followed in summer by clusters of small, round, scented blooms in shades of purple, pink, red, or white; some are bicolored. Plant this colorful perennial in groups for the best effect and stake tall varieties to keep plants upright. Remove faded flower stems in the fall and mulch plants in spring.

'Franz Schubert' produces tall stems of pearly-pink flowers loved by bees in late summer.

NINEBARK *PHYSOCARPUS OPULIFOLIUS*

HEIGHT AND SPREAD up to 8 × 6½ ft (2.5 × 2 m)
SOIL Well-drained
HARDINESS Zones 3–7
SUN ☀ ☀

Grown primarily for its colorful lobed foliage, this deciduous shrub is also studded with domed clusters of small pink-tinted white flowers in early summer. The blooms, which are loved by bees, are followed by red seed heads that add further interest. Choose 'Diabolo' for dark purple foliage, or 'Dart's Gold' for bright golden spring leaves that fade to green. 'Little Angel' is a dwarf form, growing to just 3¼ ft (1 m) in height and spread. Prune after flowering in summer.

The dark burgundy leaves of 'Diabolo' are matched with clusters of small, pollen-rich, white flowers in early summer.

LUNGWORT *PULMONARIA*

HEIGHT AND SPREAD 12 × 12 in (30 × 30 cm)
SOIL Moist but well-drained
HARDINESS Zones 3–9
SUN ☀ ☀

Lungwort is a decorative shade-loving evergreen perennial that will brighten up dark corners with its rough, hairy leaves and sprays of dainty bell-shaped blue, purple, or pink spring flowers, which bumblebees adore. Some forms sport spotted, marbled, or silvery foliage, adding to this plant's charms, while others, including 'Raspberry Splash' and 'Mrs. Moon', feature pink and blue flowers on the same plant. Wear gloves to remove old foliage in spring, after the plants have bloomed.

'Raspberry Splash' combines spotted foliage with pink flowers that turn purple and blue.

PLANTING FOR VERTICAL SURFACES

Using climbers to cover walls, fences, pergolas, and arches in a small yard or on a terrace or balcony delivers an array of colorful flowers and lush leaves, while taking up little ground space and leaving room for furniture and other plants to create a rich, layered look. However, choose your climbers with care, as some, often described as "vigorous," may require frequent pruning to prevent them from engulfing your garden. Look carefully at the descriptions and heights and spreads of your chosen plants to ensure they will suit the space available.

PLANTING UP VERTICAL FEATURES

Enhancing your space with climbing plants is easy, but there are a few factors to consider before you start. First, check the method by which your plant climbs

After planting a climber, tie the flexible stems along a series of horizontal wires to cover a fence or wall.

(see right), which will determine the type of support it requires or if it can ascend a structure unaided. Also read the information on final heights and spreads, to make sure that those you like are suitable for their intended purpose. However, don't be put off by potentially tall plants, since most climbers can be trained horizontally as well as vertically; for example, a rose that reaches 20 ft (6 m) in height can be grown along a wall 5 ft (1.5 m) tall and 20 ft (6 m) long. Plant at least 2 ft (60 cm) away from a fence, screen, or wall, or slightly farther away from a tree trunk, as the soil close to these features will be very dry and your plant may struggle to establish.

Avoid fast-growing plants, such as mile-a-minute (*Fallopia baldschuanica*), which, as its name suggests, will grow very rapidly and may need cutting back regularly to keep it in check. Also avoid large, heavy-limbed climbers such as wisteria, unless you have a strong support for it to scale and are prepared to prune it twice a year in summer and winter to keep its wayward stems under control. A list of more suitable choices can be found on pp.70–73.

HOW PLANTS CLIMB

Climbers use a range of methods to haul themselves up, so check which one your proposed plant employs and install an appropriate support for it to ascend.

TWINING TENDRILS AND STEMS Twining climbers include plants such as clematis and passion flowers that use leaf stalks and tendrils to cling to their supports. Honeysuckle (*Lonicera*) and star jasmine (*Trachelospermum*) have twining stems that wrap around a support. Both types need wires, trellis, canes, or a shrub or tree to climb up.

HOOKS Climbing and rambling roses ascend by hooking their thorny stems onto shrubs and trees. Trellis and wires can also be used as supports but the rose stems will need to be tied on to them each year to keep them in place. Ramblers will climb unaided up a tree once the stems reach the lower branches.

STEM ROOTS AND ADHESIVE PADS Plants such as ivy, Boston ivy, and Virginia creeper (*Parthenocissus* species), and climbing hydrangea (*H. anomala* subsp. *petiolaris*) employ either stem roots or adhesive pads to cling to their supports and require no additional supports to climb up a structure.

This trellis is a short distance from the wall, allowing the twining stems of a passion flower to grip it.

> TOP TIP PLANTING A CLIMBER OVER A WOODEN STRUCTURE CAN HELP PROTECT THE TIMBER FROM WEATHERING, THEREBY REDUCING THE NEED TO APPLY PRESERVATIVES OR PAINT—BUT BE WARY OF SELF-CLINGING TYPES, SUCH AS IVY, WHICH MAY UNDERMINE OLD OR CRACKED POINTING IN BRICKWORK.

INSTALLING TRELLIS

When attaching a support to a vertical structure such as a wall or fence, make sure that it will take the weight of a mature plant—the stems of shrubby climbers such as roses or *Clematis montana* can be heavy. Also check that there is space around the support to allow the stems or tendrils to twine and grip it. To achieve this with a trellis panel, screw two horizontal wooden battens top and bottom to a wall or fence and attach the trellis to them.

Create a gap behind a trellis by screwing two wooden battens to a wall before attaching the panel to them.

Install two screw eyes at the same height up a fence panel and run sturdy garden wire between them, securing it as shown.

HOW TO WIRE UP A SURFACE

Lines of sturdy horizontal wires affixed to your structure at intervals of about 12 in (30 cm) make ideal supports for twining climbers and climbing roses. Tensioned wire trellis kits, which comprise stainless steel wires attached to durable mounts, are a good choice for large climbers, or you can buy heavy-duty garden wire and attach it to screw eyes installed into a wall or fence, or vertically up the posts of an arch or pergola. Simply twist the wire around one screw eye and stretch it across to a second one, then insert the wire and twist to secure it. Repeat until the whole structure is wired up.

PLANTS FOR VERTICAL SURFACES

By selecting a range of seasonal climbers, you can transform your walls, fences, pergolas, and arches into veils of foliage and flowers all year round. You can also plant a couple, such as clematis and a climbing rose, about a yard (meter) apart and leave them to intertwine for double the color. Just remember that most of these plants will require extra supports to scramble up (*see p.68–69*) and sufficient space to expand.

COMMON HOP *HUMULUS LUPULUS*

HEIGHT AND SPREAD up to 20 × 20 ft (6 × 6 m)
SOIL Moist but well-drained
HARDINESS Zones 4–8
SUN ☼ ☼

This fast-growing perennial twining climber will quickly cover a fence or wall every year with its large decorative green leaves, which drop in the fall and return each spring. In summer, green flowers appear, followed by papery seed heads, or hops, which are the parts used in brewing. For more vibrant color, try the golden-leaved 'Aureus'. Hops are easy to grow, just requiring a support for their rambling stems to curl around. Cut plants back during the summer if they outgrow their space.

The hops are the seed heads that appear in early fall and are used in brewing.

CLIMBING HYDRANGEA

HYDRANGEA ANOMALA SUBSP. *PETIOLARIS*

HEIGHT AND SPREAD up to 50 × 10 ft (15 × 3 m)
SOIL Well-drained
HARDINESS Zones 4–9
SUN ☼ ☼ ☼

Perfect for a shady small space, this reliable climber needs no wires or trellis to scramble up a wall or fence, its woody stems clinging via aerial roots. Loved for its lacy white flowers, which appear throughout summer, the dark green heart-shaped leaves turn yellow before dropping in the fall. Very easy to grow, this hydrangea will thrive in most soils and sun as well as shade. Leave it to ramble or prune after flowering to keep it in check.

Starry white flowers form a lacy effect in summer and attract a host of pollinators.

COMMON HONEYSUCKLE *LONICERA PERICLYMENUM*

HEIGHT AND SPREAD 22 × 6½ ft (7 × 2 m)
SOIL Moist but well-drained
HARDINESS Zones 4–9
SUN ☼

The common honeysuckle is a stalwart of cottage-style gardens, decorating walls, fences, and arches with its twining stems of highly fragrant white, yellow, red, or pink flowers, which stand out against lush green leaves. The summer blooms are followed by glossy red berries that add to the show. Plant this climber close to a seating area or in an area where you can enjoy the scent. It grows in any reasonable soil and will lose its leaves in winter. Prune in late winter or early spring.

'Serotina' produces two-tone red-and-white flowers followed by bright red berries.

CLEMATIS *CLEMATIS* SPECIES

Colorful clematis offer interest throughout the year, and while some varieties will climb into a treetop, others are perfect for patio pots. These twining plants are grouped by their flowering times and pruning needs; all are easy to care for, requiring little attention once established.

HEIGHT AND SPREAD Up to 20 × 15 ft (6 × 5 m)
SOIL Moist but well-drained
HARDINESS Zones 4–9
SUN ☼ ☼

GROUP ONE

Clematis in Group One comprise winter- and early spring-flowering plants. They include evergreens, such as *C. cirrhosa*, which are best suited to a sheltered city space, and the vigorous and hardier white- or pink- flowered *C. montana* that will cover a boundary fence with ease. Smaller clematis in this group include the alpina and macropetala types, which are fully hardy and produce dainty nodding flowers in colors ranging from purple and blue to pink and white. Plant the stems deeply, burying them about 2 in (5 cm) below the surface. Prune these plants only to control their size; trim lightly immediately after flowering.

GROUP TWO

Large-flowered clematis hybrids that bloom in early summer make up Group Two. Favorites include the pink-striped 'Nelly Moser', purple-blue 'The President', and elegant white 'Snow Queen'. For shady sites, try the rich, claret-red 'Niobe', which thrives in lower light. Plant the stems deeply (see Group One) and prune annually in late winter or early spring. Group Two clematis bloom on the previous year's growth. Prune established plants lightly in early spring, cutting above the first healthy bud from the top of each stem. Prune new plants hard in spring to encourage more stems to form (this will reduce flowering until next year).

Clematis tangutica offers yellow flowers and fluffy seed heads in the fall.

GROUP THREE

The clematis in Group Three flower in late summer and early fall. They include the tall *C. tangutica*, with nodding bell-like flowers followed by long-lasting fluffy seed heads; 'Étoile Violette', with small but profuse dark purple flowers; and the range of clematis bred by Raymond Evison for growing in pots. This diverse group, labeled as Evison or Evipo clematis, are prized for their abundant blooms and disease resistance. Plant deeply (see Group One) and prune annually in late winter or early spring. These clematis flower on the current season's growth and all stems should be cut to a pair of leaf buds about 1 ft (30 cm) above soil level.

'Frances Rivis' is an alpina clematis with nodding purple and white spring blooms.

'Niobe' is a rich red-flowered Group Two clematis that will thrive in shade.

ROSES

Offering unbeatable fragrance and flower colors, many climbing and rambling roses are ideally suited to small gardens. Use them to decorate pergolas, arches, walls, and fences, but choose carefully: some ramblers will easily scale a mature tree, while climbers are often more compact.

HEIGHT AND SPREAD Ramblers: up to 70 × 20 ft (20 × 6 m); Climbers: up to 20 × 3¼ ft (6 × 1 m)
SOIL Moist but well-drained
HARDINESS Zones 5–9
SUN ☼ ☼

'Félicité Perpétue' produces a single but spectacular flush of creamy-white flowers in midsummer.

Award-winning 'Constance Spry' carries rich pink blooms with a sweet scent in early summer.

RAMBLING ROSES

These large rose plants produce long, sturdy stems that can reach up into the canopy of a tall tree within a few years. Most produce one flush of flowers each year and they are perfect for papering the walls or fences of a small space, where their abundant little flowers will produce a glorious display in late spring or summer. However, while some grow no more than 12 ft (4 m), most are too large for a balcony. Among the best ramblers are the white 'Félicité Perpétue', with its fragrant pompom flowers; the creamy-yellow 'Albéric Barbier'; and the fragrant white and pale pink 'Francis E. Lester'. Prune lightly after flowering.

CLIMBING ROSES

Generally smaller than ramblers, some climbing roses will produce a succession of flowers from summer to early fall, especially if you deadhead the blooms as they fade. Buy a short one such as 'Gertrude Jekyll' or 'Blush Noisette' for a trellis, or larger climbers, including the scented rich pink 'Constance Spry', pearly pink 'New Dawn', or fragrant cream 'Mme Alfred Carrière', to cover an arch or pergola. Climbers flower on stems produced the previous year and should be pruned in early spring (see also p.132). Train the stems in a fan shape or along horizontal wires to encourage the most abundant flower displays.

CLIMBERS FOR SHADE

Climbers that tolerate shade are particularly useful for small town gardens overshadowed by surrounding buildings. While most climbing roses are best grown in sun, ramblers tolerate more shade, since they are adapted to growing through dense tree canopies. Look out also for climbing roses that have been bred for shadier spots. The fragrant pink 'Mme Grégoire Staechelin' is suitable for a shady wall and while it only flowers once, the blooms are followed by large red hips that extend the interest. 'Mme Alfred Carrière', 'Constance Spry', and the golden flowers of 'Maigold' will also thrive in low light conditions.

The golden flowers of climber *Rosa* 'Maigold' bloom well in partial shade.

CHILEAN POTATO VINE *SOLANUM CRISPUM*

HEIGHT AND SPREAD 12 × 5 ft (4 × 1.5 m)
SOIL Moist but well-drained
HARDINESS Zones 9–11
SUN ☼

Given a warm, sheltered spot, this semi-evergreen twining climber will reward you with clusters of small purple blooms through summer and early fall. Small, cream, poisonous berries follow the flowers, and in areas protected from frost, this climber may also retain its slim green leaves over winter. 'Glasnevin' is a popular cultivar, or opt for the white-flowered 'Album'. To maintain your vine, trim back the side stems to two or three healthy buds from the main stems in spring.

The pretty purplish-blue flowers of the potato vine bloom throughout summer.

BLACK-EYED SUSAN *THUNBERGIA ALATA*

HEIGHT AND SPREAD 6½ × 1¾ ft (2 × 0.5 m)
SOIL Well-drained
HARDINESS Zones 9–11
SUN ☼

Famous for its colorful flowers in shades of yellow, orange, and pink, each with a distinctive black center, this compact annual climber is a great choice for growing up a tripod or over a trellis screen. The heart-shaped leaves offer a good foil for the flowers, which bloom from summer to early fall. It is easy to grow from seed, or buy young seedlings in late spring. Plant out after the frosts in well-drained soil or pots filled with peat-free commercial potting mix. Keep plants well watered during dry spells.

Thunbergia alata **'Lemon'** produces clear yellow blooms with dark eyes in summer.

STAR JASMINE *TRACHELOSPERMUM JASMINOIDES*

HEIGHT AND SPREAD up to 26 × 20 ft (8 × 6 m)
SOIL Well-drained
HARDINESS Zones 8–10
SUN ☼ ☼

A must-have climber for a small town space, the star jasmine's twining stems of evergreen foliage and tiny but highly scented white summer flowers make the perfect leafy cover for a fence or wall. The leaves turn deep bronze-red in winter, adding to this plant's charms. The only proviso is that it needs a sheltered site and will not tolerate very low winter temperatures, cold winds, or wet soils. Star jasmine rarely needs pruning, but you can remove weak or damaged stems in spring.

Star jasmine is loved for its evergreen foliage and highly scented flowers.

FLAME FLOWER *TROPAEOLUM SPECIOSUM*

HEIGHT AND SPREAD up to 10 × 3¼ ft (3 × 1 m)
SOIL Moist but well-drained
HARDINESS Zones 8–11
SUN ☼ ☼

Despite its tropical looks, this colorful, well-behaved perennial climber is hardy in most areas, producing its slender stems of cloverlike leaves and long-spurred bright scarlet flowers all summer. It then puts on its fall show of sapphire-blue berries. Use it to cover walls and fences, or grow it on a large trellis on a balcony. It will also scramble through evergreen shrubs. Provide it with a sheltered spot where the roots will be in shade in summer. While slow to establish, it's worth the wait.

The flame flower will enliven any small outdoor space with its bright flowers.

PLANTING A PATIO GARDEN

A small paved or gravel patio offers a wealth of planting opportunities that can make a pocket-size space feel more like a full-size yard. Provide year-round color by combining a range of different plants and flowers, using their foliage and blooms to create a long period of seasonal interest. Plan the role of each of your plants and ensure they are planted in the right type of container, whether they are designed to inject pops of transient flower color or create a more permanent presence.

Rendered raised beds allow space for layers of leafy structural plants, including a *Fatsia*, hostas, and *Miscanthus* grass.

RAISING YOUR GAME

Surrounding a patio with raised beds will provide both height and a good depth of soil to home a selection of evergreens and colorful flowers to create a long season of interest. Try combining a small deciduous tree such as a Japanese maple (*Acer palmatum*) with evergreens shrubs that offer year-round interest, including *Euonymus*, *Fatsia*, and Japanese holly (*Ilex crenata*). If there is space, include a few perennial and annual flowering plants and bulbs to provide colorful highlights as the seasons turn. Raised beds also make good homes for a few herbs to add to the barbecue, and edibles such as lettuces, green onions, and radishes.

Soil and water will escape from the base of a bed made from a self-assembly kit, so a patio of light-colored stone paving may become stained around it, unless you pull up slabs under the bed to allow moisture to drain into the ground. A framework of brick walls is another, more solid option. Never build the walls over, or pile up soil next to, a damp course around the house, and always include drainage at the base of the bed to prevent plants becoming waterlogged.

FLEXIBLE FOCUS

Planting in pots offers greater flexibility than a raised bed, since you can move small or light containers around as required. While large trees and shrubs in heavy vessels are best planted and left in situ, pots of spring bulbs, summer bedding, or perennial plants such as heucheras, penstemons, and fuchsias can be rotated, so that they provide the focus of your display when in bloom. Select from the plant suggestions on pp.78–81, 84–87, and 90–93, and remember to raise containers up on "pot feet" or bricks to allow water to drain from the base.

Slip a small pot filled with annuals such as begonias into the top of an urn for a tall, light feature that's easy to move.

WALL-TO-WALL COLOR

Climbers are a great option for a patio garden, allowing you to make the most of the wall or fence space surrounding it (see pp.68–73). Most perennial and shrubby climbers are more likely to thrive if you plant them in a raised bed or a strip of soil in the ground rather than a pot, which they may outgrow in a year or two. If you only have space for a container, however, consider planting

an annual climber such as sweet peas, purple bell vine (*Rhodochiton*), or black-eyed susan (*Thunbergia alata*), which will grow well in a large pot, given a support of wires, trellis, or canes to scramble up (see pp.68–69).

Wall pots and hanging baskets offer another planting solution for the boundaries around a patio. Try small spring bulbs followed by drought-resistant plants such as pelargoniums in pots, or fill hanging baskets with seasonal bedding—those with closed sides are easier to maintain because they retain more water (see also p.83 for tips on installing brackets for baskets).

Affix lightweight planters to a fence and fill with annuals and trailers such as silver *Dichondra* and lime-green *Ipomoea batatas*.

PLANTING IN PAVING

Plants in the ground tend to need watering less frequently than those in pots, so consider pulling up a paving stone to create an instant flowerbed.

YOU WILL NEED Mallet and chisel • Crowbar or garden fork • Spade • Garden topsoil or compost • Plant (*Phormium* used here) • All-purpose granular fertilizer • Decorative stones or gravel (optional)

1 Using the mallet and chisel, remove any grouting around your chosen paving stone, then carefully lift it out with a crowbar or garden fork. Remove the sand and concrete beneath the slab and dig a hole a little deeper than the plant's root ball. Add some garden topsoil or compost to the hole.
2 Water your plant thoroughly about 30 minutes before planting. Add it to the hole, ensuring that the root ball will be at the same level once planted as it was in its original pot. Apply some granular fertilizer at the rate recommended on the packaging.
3 Fill in around the plant with more soil or compost and firm in with your hands to remove large air gaps. Water the plant well.

4 Ideally, add some decorative stones or gravel over the soil surface to help lock moisture in the soil and prevent weed growth. Continue to water the plant during dry periods until you see new growth emerge. When the plant is well established, water only during prolonged dry spells or if it is wilting.

PLANTING A CONTAINER

Follow these simple steps to create a permanent display of ferns in a pot for a shady area, where they will overwinter outside. The method is just the same for planting up a sun-loving summer container or a window box for a sill or balcony. Choose a commercial potting mix for plants that will be in their pots for just a few months, or mix in sterilized topsoil for plants that will remain in situ for a few years (see also potting mixes for balconies on p.82).

Shade-loving ferns provide a leafy year-round display for a cool spot, where they work well alongside pots of fuchsias.

MAKE A FERN MEDLEY

Perfect for a cool spot, this group of ferns will be happy for a couple years in their container before they will need to be repotted.

YOU WILL NEED Frost-proof terra-cotta pot, 12–18 in (30–45 cm) wide • Broken pot pieces • Commercial potting mix plus added topsoil • Slow-release fertilizer (optional) • Crested hart's tongue (*Asplenium scolopendrium* Cristata Group) • Japanese painted fern (*Athyrium niponicum* var. *pictum*) • Shield fern (*Polystichum makinoi*)

1 Source a frost-proof terra-cotta pot 12–18 in (30–45 cm) in diameter and deep enough to accommodate the ferns' root balls. Place some broken pot pieces over the drainage holes to prevent them clogging up with soil and impeding drainage.
2 Add a layer of potting mix, and if it does not contain fertilizer, apply some slow-release granules at the rate recommended on the packaging.
3 Water the ferns well before planting. Slip them out of their containers and add them to the pot. Fill in around the root balls with more potting mix.
4 Firm down the potting mix around the roots, checking that there are no gaps between them—the roots will dry out

if they are not covered. Water well and keep the potting mix moist from spring to fall. *Athyrium* is deciduous and will die down in the fall, but new leaves will appear the following spring.

TOP TIP IN SPRING, REMOVE THE TOP LAYER OF POTTING MIX CAREFULLY, ENSURING YOU DO NOT DAMAGE THE ROOTS, AND REPLACE IT WITH SOME ALL-PURPOSE GRANULAR FERTILIZER MIXED WITH FRESH POTTING MIX.

CREATE A POT
OF SUMMER FLOWERS

Containers bursting with summer flowers deliver color all summer until the tender types are killed by frost. Follow the steps opposite to create your display, using any good commercial potting mix.

Include in your display a combination of tall plants such as tobacco plants and penstemons in the center, and shorter bedding, including petunias and dwarf osteospermums, around the edges. Finally, squeeze in a few trailing plants to spill over the sides of the pot. The white cascading plants here are bacopa, but you could use surfinia petunias or calibrachoas (see p.97). Do not be tempted to put your tender summer flowers outside until all risk of frost has passed in late spring. The blooms will last until the fall.

These summer bedding plants all require at least six hours of direct sun each day to bloom well.

PLANTS FOR PATIOS

Create a lush green space on your patio with plants in containers and, if you have space, beds around the edges, combining structural evergreen shrubs with seasonal blooms to produce a colorful year-round display. Many of the choices here will grow well in the shade of surrounding buildings, and you can mix and match them with the plants recommended for balconies (*see pp.84–87*). In sunny spots, you could include a few pots of herbs, some soft fruits, and salad crops such as tomatoes and peppers (*see pp.102–109*) in the mix.

JAPANESE MAPLE *ACER PALMATUM*

HEIGHT AND SPREAD up to 12 × 12 ft (4 × 4 m) in a pot
SOIL Moist but well-drained
HARDINESS Zones 5–9
SUN ☼ ☼

Few trees grow as well in pots as Japanese maples. Loved for their colorful lobed leaves and spectacular fall color, these slow-growing plants will thrive in a large container filled with potting mix and topsoil, given enough moisture, or grow them in the ground if you have space. Choose a spot in part shade, where the foliage is less likely to dry out in hot summers. Apply an all-purpose granular fertilizer to a potted tree each spring. See p.52 for some good cultivar choices.

The graceful structure and colorful leaves of Japanese maples create a striking display.

AFRICAN LILY *AGAPANTHUS*

HEIGHT AND SPREAD up to 3¼ × 3¼ ft (1 × 1 m)
SOIL Well-drained
HARDINESS Zones 8–10
SUN ☼

The large, spherical blue or white flower heads of this strappy-leaved perennial make a striking feature in a pot or border when they appear in late summer and early fall. For a patio, select a hardy deciduous agapanthus that can be left outside all year—evergreen types will need winter protection in cold areas. You can also buy dwarf varieties such as 'Lilliput' that reach just 16 in (40 cm) in height. Potted plants will need an all-purpose granular fertilizer once a year in spring.

'Northern Star' produces an abundance of dark violet-blue flowers in summer and fall.

COSMOS *COSMOS BIPINNATUS*

HEIGHT AND SPREAD up to 5 ft × 20 in (1.5 × 0.5 m)
SOIL Moist but well-drained
HARDINESS Zones 2–11
SUN ☼

Prized for their delicate ferny foliage and large daisylike flowers, cosmos are a must for any sunny patio garden. Choose tall types that flower on sturdy stems to surround a seating area with blooms or, for small pots, opt for the dwarf Sonata Series, which reach just 12 in (30 cm) in height. These annuals are easy to grow from seed, or buy young plug plants in spring, and plant them out after the frosts. Deadhead the blooms regularly and they should continue to flower into the fall.

'Psyche White' has tall stems of semi-double flowers that will add impact to a seating area.

DAHLIA *DAHLIA (DWARF)*

HEIGHT AND SPREAD up to 24 × 24 in (60 × 60 cm)
SOIL Well-drained
HARDINESS Zones 3–11
SUN ☼

While border dahlias can produce towering stems of 4 ft (1.2 m) or more that often need staking, the dwarf types are easy-care plants designed for patio pots. Try the Happy Series, which reach just 12 in (30 cm) and produce colorful anemone-shaped flowers against dark purple foliage, or opt for a tiny ball dahlia with pompom blooms, or dwarf cactus-flowered plants, which look like exploding fireworks. Keep the soil moist and feed with a high-potash fertilizer if plants start to flag in late summer.

The Happy Series of dahlias offer long-lasting summer flowers above dark foliage.

MEXICAN FLEABANE *ERIGERON KARVINSKIANUS*

HEIGHT AND SPREAD 8 × 20 in (20 × 50 cm)
SOIL Well-drained
HARDINESS Zones 6–9
SUN ☼ ☼

Once planted, never forgotten, this diminutive perennial is a prolific self-seeder, naturalizing wherever it finds a foothold between cracks in patio paving or along the edges of a border. Alternatively, use it to spill from the sides of a container. It produces mats of narrow leaves and dainty white daisylike flowers that turn to pink, appearing from late spring to late fall. It could be classed as a weed for its wandering ways but the flowers are so pretty that most people just let it be.

Mexican fleabane's dainty white daisies mature to pink to create a pretty duo-tone effect.

JAPANESE SPINDLE *EUONYMUS JAPONICUS*

HEIGHT AND SPREAD up to 12 × 12 ft (4 × 4 m)
SOIL Well-drained/moist but well-drained
HARDINESS Zones 6–9
SUN ☼ ☼

Create a leafy backdrop for flowering plants with the dark green oval leaves of this bushy evergreen shrub. Grow it in a large pot if you want to restrict its size and choose the plain green species for shady sites. Where there's more light, try 'Microphyllus Albovariegatus' with its elegant white-edged green leaves, or 'Microphyllus Aureovariegatus', which has yellow-variegated foliage with reddish-bronze tints in winter. Feed potted plants with an all-purpose granular fertilizer each spring.

Hardy and tolerant of drought, Japanese spindle provides color year-round.

HARDY FUCHSIA *FUCHSIA*

HEIGHT AND SPREAD up to 5 × 5 ft (1.5 × 1.5 m)
SOIL Well-drained/moist but well-drained
HARDINESS Zones 6–7
SUN ☼ ☼

Fuchsias are useful for shady patios, flowering well if given just a few hours of sun each day in summer. Choose the hardy types if you have no space to store your plants indoors over winter. The large *Fuchsia magellanica* is a good choice for a border and produces small, dainty flowers from midsummer. There is also a wide choice of smaller plants with bigger blooms that are suitable for pots. Trim old growth back to a healthy bud in spring and apply an all-purpose granular fertilizer at the same time.

'Brutus' is a hardy fuchsia with cascading stems of crimson and pinky-purple flowers.

JAPANESE HOLLY *ILEX CRENATA*

HEIGHT AND SPREAD 12 × 3¼ ft (4 × 1 m)
SOIL Well-drained/moist but well-drained
HARDINESS Zones 5–7
SUN ☼ ☼

The small, glossy, evergreen leaves of this slow-growing shrub look very similar to those of boxwood (*Buxus*), which is now rarely planted since falling prey to pests and diseases. Use Japanese holly instead for topiary and hedging, or leave it unchecked to produce its small white summer flowers and black fruits. It will grow well in a large pot, or plant a few in a border to enclose a seating area and provide shelter. Feed potted plants with an all-purpose granular fertilizer in spring.

Japanese holly's small, smooth-edged leaves can be clipped to create topiary or a low evergreen hedge.

SPOTTED DEADNETTLE *LAMIUM MACULATUM*

HEIGHT AND SPREAD 4 × 20 in (10 × 50 cm)
SOIL Well-drained/moist but well-drained
HARDINESS Zones 3–8
SUN ☼ ☼

The sprawling stems of this evergreen perennial form a carpet of leafy growth and purple, white, or pink flowers in summer. Use it as ground cover around the edges of a patio, or allow the leafy stems to trail from the sides of a pot. The pale green foliage, sometimes variegated with white patterns, provides winter interest and combines successfully with small shrubs and violas in containers. Trim overly long stems in spring and feed potted plants with an all-purpose granular fertilizer at the same time.

Shade-loving deadnettle creates a frilly edge around pots, or can be used as ground cover.

TOBACCO PLANT *NICOTIANA ALATA*

HEIGHT AND SPREAD 24 × 12 in (60 × 30 cm)
SOIL Well-drained/moist but well-drained
HARDINESS Zones 3–10
SUN ☼ ☼

These tender perennials are usually grown as annuals, and will decorate a pot or border around a patio with their spoon-shaped dark green leaves and evening-scented flowers. The trumpet-shaped blooms are available in a wide range of colors, including lime green, white, pink, and red, and plants flower continuously from summer to early fall. Plant them around a seating area, where they will perfume the evening air. For taller plants, try *Nicotiana mutabilis* or *N. sylvestris*.

The evening-scented flowers of a tobacco plant will perfume the air around a seating or dining area.

OSMANTHUS *OSMANTHUS × BURKWOODII*

HEIGHT AND SPREAD up to 8 × 8 ft (2.5 × 2.5 m)
SOIL Well-drained
HARDINESS Zones 6–8
SUN ☼ ☼

An evergreen shrub with dark green glossy foliage, osmanthus offers year-round color and structure and provides a backdrop for more colorful flowers on a patio. In spring it also produces clusters of small, highly scented white flowers, occasionally followed by a few black fruits. When grown in the ground, it will develop into a large shrub, but confining it to a pot will limit its size. Feed potted plants with an all-purpose granular fertilizer in spring, and prune after they have flowered.

The scented, jasmine-like flowers of this drought-tolerant shrub appear in spring along the leafy stems.

PENSTEMON *PENSTEMON*

HEIGHT AND SPREAD up to 3 × 1 ft (90 × 30 cm)
SOIL Well-drained
HARDINESS Zones 4–9
SUN ☼ ☀

This long-flowering perennial makes a splash on a patio with its spikes of tubular, foxglove-like flowers, which appear from summer to early fall above small green leaves. Choose from the wide range of colors, which include white, pink, red, and purple, or opt for a bi-colored plant. Plants will overwinter outside in a sheltered garden, but move them inside in cold areas or cover with a few layers of horticultural fleece. Feed potted plants in spring with all-purpose granular fertilizer.

'Raven' produces dark purple flowers with white throats and will grow well in a pot or bed.

PATIO ROSE *ROSA* (PATIO SHRUB ROSE)

HEIGHT AND SPREAD up to 24 × 24 in (60 × 60 cm)
SOIL Well-drained/moist but well-drained
HARDINESS Zones 4–9
SUN ☼

As the name suggests, these diminutive roses have been bred for growing in patio pots and window boxes. They come in the same color range as full-size roses, while some, including 'Flower Power Gold', 'Little Sunset', and 'White Patio', are lightly fragrant. Many grow little more than 12 in (30 cm) in height and are perfect for injecting color into sunny areas, where they will bloom all summer if deadheaded regularly. Feed in spring with an all-purpose granular fertilizer.

The **'Sweet'** series of roses such as the pale orange 'Sweet Dream' has been bred to thrive in pots.

HOUSELEEK *SEMPERVIVUM*

HEIGHT AND SPREAD up to 4 × 4 in (10 × 10 cm)
SOIL Well-drained
HARDINESS Zones 4–8
SUN ☼ ☀

Ideal for squeezing between paving slabs and decorating tiny pots, these small evergreen perennials create a mat of textured foliage in colors ranging from bright green to dark purple and red. Stout little stems topped with starry flowers push up through the leafy rosettes in summer, after which the foliage dies, but plants usually put on new growth to replace any that's lost. Houseleeks require good drainage, and half the recommended dose of granular fertilizer in spring.

The common houseleek is fully hardy and produces dainty rosettes of small, spiny leaves.

JAPANESE SKIMMIA *SKIMMIA JAPONICA*

HEIGHT AND SPREAD up to 30 × 30 in (75 × 75 cm)
SOIL Moist but well-drained
HARDINESS Zones 6–8
SUN ☼ ☀

This compact evergreen shrub with dark green, leathery leaves is a good choice for a shady patio. Skimmias are dioecious, which means that the male and female flowers are produced on different plants. Male plants bear cone-shaped heads of white or red buds in winter, followed by white flowers; the females produce red fall and winter berries, as well as spring flowers, but you will need a male to pollinate them. Feed in spring with an all-purpose granular fertilizer.

'Rubella' is a male skimmia that produces decorative red flower buds in winter.

PLANTING A BALCONY

Using plants to decorate the walls and floor space on your balcony will envelop you in a lush landscape of foliage, flowers, and herbs to enjoy all year round from inside and out. Pack planters, wall pots, and hanging baskets with a combination of evergreen shrubs and perennials for permanent color and interest, and bulbs and bedding to provide seasonal highlights as the months pass.

Plant flowers and edibles in a green wall pocket system to maximize the planting area on your balcony.

SAFETY FIRST

When you create a garden on a balcony, the pots and containers, plus potting mix, plants, and water, can substantially increase the weight and possibly affect the safety of the structure. Bearing this in mind, select lightweight planters and furniture, and if you want to include more than a few pots, it may also be wise to consult a chartered structural engineer or a surveyor to check that your planned planting scheme will be safe. Also ensure that balustrades are secure and, again, call in professional help if you are in any doubt.

Plant in lightweight containers so displays do not exceed the load-bearing capacity.

A deep planter and modern trellis provide a home for *Thunbergia* vines and edible plants, including squashes.

SELECTING POTS AND PLANTS

Choose a variety of lightweight containers for your balcony, and make sure that once planted they will be secure and strong winds will not lift them off, endangering people below. This may mean screwing them to a wall. Planters made from galvanized steel, synthetic materials (upcycled plastic pots will help to minimize pollution levels), treated wood, or bamboo are all good options for large displays, while small terra-cotta pots can be used to home succulents or a few bedding plants. Make sure any planters you use have drainage holes in the bottom and put them on

bricks or pot "feet" to allow water to escape easily. To maximize your use of space, plant up your wall, too. Hanging baskets or green wall systems can be used for flowers, salad leaves, and small herbs. You could also plant a climber in a pot and train it up trellis or wires fixed to a wall.

Select plants from those on pp.84–87, 90–93, and 96–99, checking that your choices suit the levels of sunlight the balcony receives. Plant in peat-free potting mix (with topsoil if needed), or a lightweight aggregate formulated for balcony and roof use, if you want large containers and plants. You can also lighten the load by putting recycled polystyrene packaging pieces in your containers before adding potting mix.

DECORATING BALUSTRADES

Containers designed to fit over balcony railings or screens offer yet more planting opportunities. Some have integrated hooks that keep them in place, while saddlebag containers made from waterproof fabric slip over the top of balustrades and provide planting pockets on either side. Plants here will receive high exposure to sun and wind and will dry out very quickly, so be prepared to water them daily in summer. Containers with integrated reservoirs in the base can help keep plants hydrated for longer periods between watering. Select plants that cope with drier soils, such as fescues, bedding verbenas, small fuchsias, begonias, pelargoniums, helichrysum, and senecio, or herbs, including chives and thyme, for these areas.

Drought-tolerant pelargoniums, silver helichrysum, and senecio are good choices for planters attached to balustrades.

HOW TO HANG A BASKET

Use sturdy brackets to secure hanging baskets to balcony walls.

YOU WILL NEED Sturdy wall bracket • Spirit level • Pencil • Electric drill with masonry bit • Anchors and coach bolts • Spanner

1 Position the wall bracket on the wall and, using a spirit level, check that it is vertical. Mark the positions of the screw holes with a pencil.
2 With the electric drill, make holes through the pencil marks, and push an anchor into each hole.
3 Put the bracket back in place, lining it up with the drilled holes. Insert a washer and coach bolt and screw it into the wall with a wrench. Repeat for the second hole, then tighten up both bolts to ensure the bracket is attached securely to the wall.
4 Add a decorative hanging basket filled with summer bedding plants or herbs, such as the thyme, tarragon, and chives shown here.

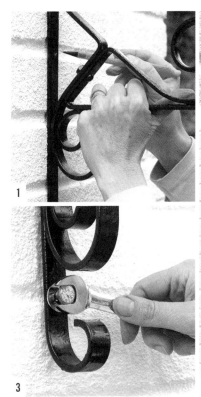

PLANTS FOR BALCONIES

With space often at a premium, planting on a balcony may be limited to wall pots or window boxes fixed to the railings, but you can still create a beautiful year-round display with a selection of evergreens, spring bulbs, and colorful summer bedding. Annual climbers are also useful, growing well in containers and covering walls or rails with a veil of foliage and flowers. Whichever plants you choose, check that their preference for sun or shade matches your aspect and that their containers have drainage at the base to prevent root rot.

BEGONIA *BEGONIA*

HEIGHT AND SPREAD up to 20 × 20 in (50 × 50 cm)
POTTING MIX Peat-free
HARDINESS Zones 9–10
SUN ☼ ☼

Bedding begonias that are bred to be grown outside during the summer months make colorful displays in pots and cope with shade as well as sun. On a sheltered balcony, they will bloom from early summer to mid-fall. Look out for trailing types with dragon-wing-shaped leaves and small flowers for a natural look or, if you're after more drama, try those with large, blowsy blooms, such as the Non-Stop Series. Semperflorens begonias have a smaller habit and are ideal for mixed flower displays.

The Starshine Series of begonias comes in a wide choice of flower colors.

JAPANESE ARALIA *FATSIA JAPONICA*

HEIGHT AND SPREAD up to 5 × 5 ft (1.5 × 1.5 m) in a pot
POTTING MIX Peat-free with added topsoil
HARDINESS Zones 8–10
SUN ☼ ☼ ☼

The bold, glossy foliage of this stately evergreen shrub offers year-round interest and provides a textured backdrop on a balcony for bright flowering plants. In early fall, it also produces spherical cream flowers that are loved by bees. A mature *Fatsia* is a large plant that will need plenty of space, but growing it in a pot will restrict its size. Apply a top-dressing of all-purpose granular fertilizer each spring to keep it healthy. You can remove any unwanted stems in late spring.

The large, glossy, lobed evergreen foliage of *Fatsia* lends a tropical note to a balcony.

BLUE FESCUE *FESTUCA GLAUCA*

HEIGHT AND SPREAD up to 12 × 12 in (30 × 30 cm)
POTTING MIX Peat-free with added topsoil
HARDINESS Zones 4–8
SUN ☼

The rounded tufts of ice-blue evergreen leaves make this little grass stand out in a container display. It also produces spikes of small blue-green flower plumes in late spring. Make sure you can offer fescues a spot in full sun, and never allow their potting mix to become wet, which may cause the roots to rot. Try 'Elijah Blue' or 'Intense Blue' for the brightest foliage. In spring, apply an all-purpose granular fertilizer and run a kitchen fork through the leaves to remove the old growth.

'Intense Blue' is a striking fescue with silvery-blue leaves that create a foil for flowers.

DWARF SUNFLOWER *HELIANTHUS ANNUUS*

HEIGHT AND SPREAD 2 × 2 ft (60 × 60 cm)
POTTING MIX Peat-free
HARDINESS Zones 3–11
SUN ☼

Guaranteed to make you smile, the distinctive yellow blooms of sunflowers will transform a balcony into a summer garden. In large, sheltered spaces, you could opt for tall plants, but the dwarf sunflowers are generally best, growing to just 2 ft (60 cm) and producing lots of smaller flowers. Try 'Munchkin' with its classic brown-eyed yellow blooms, the red-flowered 'Ms Mars', or the pompom-shaped blooms of 'Teddy Bear'. They are easy to grow from seed, or buy plug plants in spring.

'Munchkin' offers classic yellow sunflower blooms on short, leafy plants.

PLANTAIN LILY *HOSTA*

HEIGHT AND SPREAD up to 3 × 3 ft (90 × 90 cm)
POTTING MIX Peat-free with added topsoil
HARDINESS Zones 3–9
SUN ☼ ☼

Hostas are loved for their large, elegant leaves and spikes of mauve, purple, or white funnel-shaped summer flowers. Check labels for final heights and spreads to ensure your chosen plant will fit your balcony—some reach up to 3 ft (90 cm) or more, so go for a miniature plant if space is tight. Slugs adore hostas, but these plants can flourish on a balcony, protected from the pests down below. They dislike sun, so tuck them beneath shrubs such as fatsias on a bright balcony.

Hosta crispula has white-edged green leaves and spikes of pale lavender flowers.

HYDRANGEA

HYDRANGEA MACROPHYLLA (DWARF TYPES)

HEIGHT AND SPREAD up to 3¼ × 3¼ ft (1 × 1 m)
POTTING MIX Peat-free with added topsoil
HARDINESS Zones 6–9
SUN ☼ ☼

Hydrangeas are long-flowering, hardy deciduous shrubs that grow well in containers if you are prepared to water them regularly. For a balcony, select a dwarf mophead type, such as 'Masja', 'Little Pink', or 'Little Purple', which reach about 30 in (75 cm). Grow blue hydrangeas in lime-free potting mix and feed with fertilizer for acid-loving plants to retain their color. Prune stems in spring to the first healthy bud from the top.

'Masja' is a compact hydrangea with beautiful pink flowers and dark green leaves, tinted red in the fall.

GERANIUM *PELARGONIUM*

HEIGHT AND SPREAD up to 20 × 20 in (50 × 50 cm)
POTTING MIX Peat-free
HARDINESS Zones 9–12
SUN ☼ ☼

Balconies ablaze with trailing pelargoniums are a common sight in Mediterranean regions, and these plants will flower well on any sunny balcony to produce a similar effect. The upright plants are equally effective on a balcony, as are scented-leaved types, which have smaller flowers but will fill the air with their rose or lemon fragrance when you rub the foliage. Half-hardy perennials, they flower all through summer and may overwinter on a balcony if you keep their soil dry, or you can bring them inside.

The lemon-scented leaves of *Pelargonium* 'Mabel Grey' emit a delicious fragrance.

PETUNIA *PETUNIA*

HEIGHT AND SPREAD up to 12 × 20 in (30 × 50 cm)
POTTING MIX Peat-free
HARDINESS Zones 2–11
SUN ☼ ☼

The large trumpet-shaped flowers and choice of upright or trailing stems make petunias a favorite for any summer container display. The flowers come in a huge range of colors, from blue and red to white, yellow, and bi-colored. Many also have a sweet scent, which is most noticeable in the evenings. These plants require regular watering and feeding to keep them blooming, but will reward you with flowers from late spring to the first frosts and even beyond that on a sheltered balcony.

'Frenzy Blue Vein' produces weather-resistant dark and pale purple blooms all summer.

COMMON POLYPODY *POLYPODIUM VULGARE*

HEIGHT AND SPREAD 12 × 24 in (30 × 60 cm)
POTTING MIX Peat-free with added topsoil
HARDINESS Zones 6–8
SUN ☼ ☼ ☼

This compact evergreen fern produces sprays of triangular leaves that are divided into many slim leaflets. It is very adaptable to life in a pot on a balcony, where its lush green foliage will provide a foil for colorful winter, spring, and summer bedding plants. It prefers a shady site but will grow in full sun, given sufficient moisture. Plant it in a large container and it will gradually spread to fill the space if you feed it each spring with an all-purpose granular fertilizer and keep the soil moist.

Evergreen polypodies offer a year-round leafy contrast to colorful flowers.

POLYANTHUS *PRIMULA* POLYANTHUS GROUP

HEIGHT AND SPREAD 8 × 8 in (20 × 20 cm)
POTTING MIX Peat-free
HARDINESS Zones 3–8
SUN ☼

These popular evergreen bedding plants are particularly useful for winter and early spring color. The flowers appear above rough-textured oval leaves and come in a range of colors, from blue and purple to pink and white, some with patterned bi-colored petals. The leaves are prone to rotting on damp soil, so make sure pots have good drainage and remove yellowing leaves. Buy plants in bloom in the fall to flower through winter—they will then develop more flowers in spring.

Polyanthus bought in flower in the fall will continue to bloom throughout winter.

PURPLE BELL VINE *RHODOCHITON ATROSANGUINEUS*

HEIGHT AND SPREAD to 5 ft × 20 in (1.5 × 0.5 m)
POTTING MIX Peat-free
HARDINESS Zones 10–11
SUN ☼

The dainty pink and purple flowers and heart-shaped leaves that adorn the twining stems of this annual climber are guaranteed to catch the eye. Either grow it from seed or buy a young plant in spring and train it up a trellis screen or, if you have space, over a tripod in a large pot. The blooms appear over many months, from early summer to the first frosts in the fall. Simply keep the potting mix moist and feed with all-purpose liquid fertilizer every week or two from late summer to keep it flowering.

Twining stems of bell-shaped pink and purple blooms create an eye-catching balcony display.

COLEUS *SOLENOSTEMON SCUTELLARIOIDES*

HEIGHT AND SPREAD 24 × 24 in (60 × 60 cm)
POTTING MIX Peat-free
HARDINESS Zones 2–11
SUN ☼ ☼

Grown for their beautiful leaf colors, coleus produce scalloped or tooth-edged triangular foliage on square-shaped stems, and spikes of small blue flowers in summer. The leaves come in a broad spectrum of colors, from lime-green to burgundy and bright pink, many intricately patterned. Grow them on their own in pots or combine them with flowers that won't detract from the foliage. They retain their bright hues through summer and fall; apply a high-nitrogen feed if your plants start to flag.

Coleus are striking foliage plants that grow well in pots and are happy in both sun or part shade.

NASTURTIUM *TROPAEOLUM MAJUS*

HEIGHT AND SPREAD up to 3¼ × 3¼ ft (1 × 1 m)
POTTING MIX Peat-free
HARDINESS Zones 3–11
SUN ☼

The scrambling stems of nasturtiums can be used either to trail from a window box or tall pot, or to twine around railings or a trellis screen. The round foliage creates a cool foil for the bright yellow, orange, or red flowers, and both the leaves and blooms are edible, often used to give a peppery kick to salads and sandwiches. Grow nasturtiums from seed and water the plants regularly; feed them and trim the stems in late summer to encourage fresh new growth if they start to look tired.

Nasturtium's colorful flowers and green or variegated leaves are edible.

TULIP *TULIPA*

HEIGHT AND SPREAD Up to 24 × 8 in (60 × 20 cm)
POTTING MIX Peat-free with added topsoil and sand
HARDINESS Zones 3–7
SUN ☼ ☼

With thousands of tulips available, from tall, elegant lily-flowered types to the shorter Kaufmanniana and Greigii varieties and tiny species tulips such as *T. humilis* and *T. turkestanica*, they offer something for everyone. The flowers come in almost every color except blue, and will grace your balcony from mid- to late spring. Plant the bulbs in the fall and keep the pots well watered when you see signs of growth in spring, ensuring they have good drainage at the base and taking care not to overwater.

Tulipa humilis is a species tulip with dainty pink flowers that blooms reliably year after year.

GARDEN VERBENA *VERBENA RIGIDA*

HEIGHT AND SPREAD 24 × 16 in (60 × 40 cm)
POTTING MIX Peat-free with added topsoil
HARDINESS Zones 7–10
SUN ☼

The scented, bright purple or magenta flowers of this compact perennial produce a long-lasting display from early summer to early fall. These verbenas will flower year after year in pots on a sunny balcony, but may not bloom as well in shadier sites. Apply an all-purpose granular fertilizer each spring to keep them healthy. While not fully hardy, they will overwinter in mild areas; in particularly cold regions, cover the plants and pots with a few layers of horticultural fleece or some recycled bubble wrap.

The fragrant purple flowers of the garden verbena bloom from summer to fall.

UP ON THE ROOF

Create an oasis on your roof with a range of beautiful plants, using some to decorate and others to help counter the effects of wind and sun, making a more relaxing environment for you to enjoy. Choose a planting palette that offers color and texture at times when you use the terrace most frequently, and include a selection of evergreens, as well as seasonal flowers, if it's on view all year round from inside your home. The weight of your plants and containers needs to be considered, too, so that collectively they do not exceed the load-bearing capacity of your roof.

FIRST STEPS

Planting can transform a barren roof terrace, with foliage plants to shelter you from the wind, architectural trees and shrubs that will protect you from strong sun, and flowers to provide pops of color. Choose robust plants that can cope with the exposed conditions and plan carefully how you will water them and remove any pruned stems. Roof terraces are designed to withstand the weight of a few planters and people, but for any new scheme, consult a structural engineer or surveyor to check that your plans are in accordance with local regulations and will not exceed the load-bearing capacity of the roof. Also ask for professional advice on waterproofing, drainage, and irrigation systems for a large terrace to prevent damage to the properties below.

> **TOP TIP** TO CREATE A DESIGNER LOOK, SELECT A SMALL PALETTE OF PLANTS AND BUY QUITE A FEW OF THE SAME TYPE, REPEATING THEM IN DIFFERENT AREAS OF YOUR TERRACE. THIS WILL HELP UNIFY YOUR SCHEME, AND WORKS EQUALLY WELL IN SMALL AND LARGE SPACES.

Informal ornamental grasses make a great accompaniment to wooden decking, adding to the rustic effect.

Layering trees, shrubs, grasses, and perennial plants in pots and raised beds creates a colorful, all-season roof-garden display.

Choose tough sun-loving plants such as phormiums, agapanthus, and sage, which can tolerate the strong sun and high winds on a roof.

LAYERED EFFECTS

To create the best effects, take time to plan your planting scheme. Use tough evergreen shrubs such as *Brachyglottis* Dunedin Group 'Sunshine', *Escallonia*, or mock privet (*Phillyrea angustifolia*), together with tall grasses to provide shade and a windbreak around your seating areas. Next, add layers of flowering plants of different heights to inject seasonal color. Try sedums, lavender, and small species tulips and other spring bulbs to add interest at different times of the year, and fill gaps with low-growing alpine and rock-garden plants that are adapted to life at high altitudes. Drought-tolerant *Aubretia*, houseleeks (*Sempervivum*), candytuft (*Iberis sempervirens*), and storksbill (*Erodium*) will all thrive on a sunny roof and are very easy to maintain. If you have space, you can also include a few plants such as a spiky *Phormium* or hardy chusan palm (*Trachycarpus fortunei*) for dramatic effect.

ROOF PLANTING DOS AND DON'TS

DO ...

- Ensure your planting scheme doesn't exceed the load-bearing capacity of your roof.
- Make sure your containers are secure and will not blow off during a storm.
- Include tough plants that can withstand strong sun and wind.
- Water your plants frequently, since they will dry out quickly, or install an automatic watering system (see p.128).

DON'T ...

- Allow plants to block the best views from your terrace.
- Expose shade-loving plants to strong sun; tuck ferns and heucheras beneath taller plants.
- Use tall plants with stems that may snap in windy weather.
- Ignore puddles on your roof after rain or irrigating your plants. Call in professional help to create better drainage to avoid damage to the property below.

CHOOSING PLANTERS

The lightweight planters and potting mixes recommended for balconies (see p.82) will work equally well on a roof. If you rent your home, you may wish to create a plan using transportable containers—buy pots of the same style for all your plants to unify your design. If you own your property, consider built-in raised beds, which can be easier to maintain since they hold greater volumes of soil and water and the plants in them tend to need irrigating less frequently than those in pots.

Stylish lightweight pots provide the perfect home for phormiums and palms on this modern roof terrace.

PLANTS FOR ROOF GARDENS

The most important characteristic of a plant suitable for a roof garden is its ability to withstand strong sun and wind. A few tough shrubs and grasses can also serve as a practical shelterbelt, protecting seating and dining areas and making them more comfortable. You can mix and match the recommendations here with the suggestions for balconies (see pp.84–87) and other plants with adaptations that protect them from intense sun, such as small or waxy leaves, or silvery, hairy foliage. These features also make them tolerant of drought.

ROCK CRESS *AUBRETIA*

HEIGHT AND SPREAD 4 × 20 in (10 × 50 cm)
SOIL Well-drained
HARDINESS Zones 4–8
SUN ☼

This low, spreading evergreen perennial grows wild in the mountains of southeastern Europe, making it ideal as edging for a raised bed on a roof terrace, where the trailing stems of small grayish-green leaves will provide interest year round. For even more color, try 'Variegata Aurea' with its yellow-edged green leaves. In spring and early summer this little plant puts on its finest show, producing masses of small purple, red, pink, or white flowers. Trim back overly long stems after flowering.

Aubretia's cascading stems of small gray-green leaves and tiny spring flowers are perfect for a roof terrace display.

WESTERN MUGWORT *ARTEMISIA LUDOVICIANA*

HEIGHT AND SPREAD 2 × 2 ft (60 × 60 cm)
SOIL Well-drained
HARDINESS Zones 4–9
SUN ☼

Mugwort may not have the prettiest name, but its mounds of silvery tooth-edged leaves make up for that. A useful plant for a roof terrace, this perennial will bask in strong sunlight while making a beautiful foil for colorful bedding and more permanent flowers, as well as providing the latter with some shelter. Some people remove the small yellow flowers that appear in summer, since they are not very decorative. Mugwort will thrive in a large pot of potting mix with topsoil or in a raised bed.

'Silver Queen' is a popular mugwort cultivar, loved for its mound of sparkling foliage.

SENECIO *BRACHYGLOTTIS*

HEIGHT AND SPREAD Up to 5 × 5 ft (1.5 × 1.5 m)
SOIL Well-drained
HARDINESS Zones 7–10
SUN ☼

Tough yet beautiful, this evergreen shrub will create an effective windbreak on a roof, while its tolerance of dry soils makes it ideal for growing in a raised bed or large container. It will also cope with salt-laden air close to the coast. The most common form is *Brachyglottis* (Dunedin Group) 'Sunshine', which produces a mound of downy gray leaves, which are joined in summer by sunny yellow, daisylike flowers. Trim back stems that have outgrown their space in mid- to late spring.

Brachyglottis (Dunedin Group) 'Sunshine' makes a beautiful silvery windbreak.

JAPANESE SEDGE *CAREX MORROWII*

HEIGHT AND SPREAD 20 ×20 in (50 × 50 cm)
SOIL Well-drained/moist but well-drained
HARDINESS Zones 5–9
SUN ☼ ☼ ☀

The almost indestructible Japanese sedge produces a fountain of slim, grasslike evergreen leaves and spikes of brown flowers in spring. It grows well in containers and tolerates shade, making it particularly useful as a filler between other plants on a roof. Try 'Ice Dance' with its white-edged green leaves, or 'Everglow', which produces cream-edged dark green foliage that takes on orange and bronze tints in the fall and winter. Divide large clumps in fall or spring to make new plants.

'Ice Dance' sports white- and green-striped leaves and spikes of brown flowers in spring.

ROCK ROSE *CISTUS*

HEIGHT AND SPREAD up to 3¼ × 3¼ ft (1 × 1 m)
SOIL Well-drained
HARDINESS Zones 6–11
SUN ☼

Rock roses are a mainstay of drought gardens, and likewise they thrive in the hot, dry conditions up on a roof. These compact evergreen shrubs produce a mound of soft gray-green foliage, and delicate white, pink, or purple-red flowers. Although their tissue-like petals last just one day, the blooms open in succession so that the plant retains a good covering all summer. Plant a rock rose in a large container or raised bed and choose from species such as *Cistus hybridus*, *C. × purpurea* and *C. × dansereaui*.

Cistus × dansereaui
'Decumbens' has white flowers with red and yellow centers.

OLEASTER *ELAEAGNUS EBBINGEI*

HEIGHT AND SPREAD up to 8 × 8 ft (2.5 × 2.5 m)
SOIL Well-drained/moist but well-drained
HARDINESS Zones 7–9
SUN ☼ ☼

Useful as a windbreak for a seating area on a roof, this rounded evergreen shrub produces broad, leathery, dark green leaves with silvery undersides. When mature, it also develops small, fragrant white flowers in the fall. It is an easygoing plant, happy in sun or part shade, and while it can grow quite big if its roots are unrestrained in the soil, life in a large container or raised bed will limit its ambitions. However, if the stems become too long, simply prune them back in late spring.

'Gilt Edge' is a colorful oleaster with glossy, bright yellow-edged dark green leaves.

RED ESCALLONIA *ESCALLONIA RUBRA*

HEIGHT AND SPREAD up to 8 × 8 ft (2.5 × 2.5 m)
SOIL Well-drained/moist but well-drained
HARDINESS Zones 8–10
SUN ☼ ☼

Often grown as a hedge in coastal regions and areas where temperatures do not plummet too far in winter, this drought-tolerant evergreen shrub also makes a good windbreak on a roof. Its glossy green leaves and bright crimson flowers, which appear in summer and early fall, provide a decorative screen when two or three plants are combined in a raised bed. Alternatively, plant individual shrubs in large containers. Trim the stems in spring to keep it neat.

Stems of glossy evergreen foliage and crimson tubular flowers create a beautiful windbreak.

HEBE (SMALL-LEAVED) *HEBE*

HEIGHT AND SPREAD up to 3¼ × 3¼ ft (1 × 1 m)
SOIL Well-drained/moist but well-drained
HARDINESS Zones 7–11
SUN ☼ ◐

Hebes come in a wide range of shapes and sizes, but those with the smallest leaves are best for a roof terrace, since they are less likely to be damaged by winds and tend to be hardier than larger-leaved types. Good choices include *Hebe rakaiensis*, with its mound of bright green leaves and white flowers; the compact *H.* 'Wingletye', which has gray-green leaves and pale mauve flowers; and the dwarf, violet-blue-flowered *H.* 'Youngii', with dark green leaves. Hebes do not respond well to pruning.

Hebe 'Wingletye' has small, pretty gray-green leaves and spikes of mauve flowers.

ENGLISH LAVENDER *LAVANDULA ANGUSTIFOLIA*

HEIGHT AND SPREAD up to 24 × 30 in (60 × 75 cm)
SOIL Well-drained
HARDINESS Zones 5–10
SUN ☼

Sun-loving English lavender will grace a roof terrace with its purple flowers and silvery-gray foliage, both of which are fragrant. Ideally suited to a pot or raised bed are 'Hidcote', with deep violet flowers; 'Munstead', which grows to about 18 in (45 cm) and produces bluish-purple blooms; and the two-tone 'Melissa Lilac', its purple buds opening to reveal pale mauve flowers. Trim the flowering stems after they have bloomed and cut back all the stems in spring to a healthy bud or leaf.

The flowers of 'Melissa Lilac' are dark purple in bud, opening to a lighter mauve.

ICE PLANT *HYLOTELEPHIUM*

HEIGHT AND SPREAD 2 × 2 ft (60 × 60 cm)
SOIL Well-drained
HARDINESS Zones 5–9
SUN ☼

Formerly known as sedums, these fleshy-leaved perennials cope well with the strong sun on a roof, although high winds may snap their stems—this won't kill them, but try to offer shelter to avoid damage. The popular *Hylotelephium* (Herbstfreude Group) 'Herbstfreude' (syn. *Sedum* 'Autumn Joy') is a good choice, with its flat-topped salmon-pink summer flowers and dark brown seed heads; the dark bronze-purple-leaved *H. telephium* (Atropurpureum Group) is also pleasing. Cut back the old stems in spring.

Hylotelephium spectabile produces gray-green leaves and flat, pinkish-mauve flower heads.

MAIDEN GRASS *MISCANTHUS SINENSIS*

HEIGHT AND SPREAD up to 8 × 5 ft (2.5 × 1.5 m)
SOIL Well-drained/moist but well-drained
HARDINESS Zones 5–9
SUN ☼

Tall and elegant, this grass will create a veil of slender leaves on a roof terrace, providing privacy and shelter from the wind. It produces fountains of green or silvery deciduous foliage that turns orange or copper in the fall, its dried stems standing well over winter. Plumes of feathery flowers also appear in the fall. Grow it in a raised bed, and opt for a dwarf variety such as 'Kleine Silberspinne' if you want a plant that reaches just 4 ft (1.2 m) in height. Cut all the old stems down in early spring.

'Ferner Osten' produces a fountain of arching leaves and feathery red fall flowers.

CHINESE FOUNTAIN GRASS
PENNISETUM ALOPECUROIDES

HEIGHT AND SPREAD 3¼ × 3¼ ft (1 × 1 m)
SOIL Well-drained
HARDINESS Zones 5–9
SUN ☼

A good choice for a roof terrace where temperatures don't fall much below freezing, this deciduous grass forms a fountain of narrow green leaves that turn pale brown in winter. Spikes of cylindrical, brushlike green to purple flowers appear in late summer. *Pennisetum* will tolerate cold snaps in winter if its potting mix is kept dry, so move it close to the house, or cover with layers of fleece. Cut the stems back in spring.

'Hameln' produces slim, arching green leaves and long, purple-tinged flower heads in late summer.

NARROW-LEAVED MOCK PRIVET
PHILLYREA ANGUSTIFOLIA

HEIGHT AND SPREAD up to 8 × 5 ft (2.5 × 1.5 m)
SOIL Well-drained
HARDINESS Zones 6–10
SUN ☼ ☼

The dark green leaves of this drought-tolerant evergreen shrub can withstand the blustery conditions on an exposed roof terrace and it's a good choice for a coastal site, too. Clusters of small, scented, creamy-white flowers appear in late spring and early summer, followed by blue-black fruits. To use it as a windbreak, plant a few in a long, raised bed, and trim it in late spring to keep the growth neat and to a desired height.

Create a windbreak on a roof with a few narrow-leaved mock privets grown in a long raised bed.

NEW ZEALAND FLAX *PHORMIUM*

HEIGHT AND SPREAD up to 8 × 5 ft (2.5 × 1.5 m)
SOIL Well-drained/moist but well-drained
HARDINESS Zones 7–11
SUN ☼ ☼

This striking evergreen perennial produces clumps of colorful arching sword-shaped leaves that make a statement in a pot or raised bed on a roof. Tolerant of wind and sun, New Zealand flaxes come in a wide range of colors, including the striped green and gold 'Yellow Wave', bronze-green and pink 'Maori' and the dark-leaved 'Black Adder'. Remove old foliage in spring. It's easy to mistake phormiums for cordylines, since they look very similar when young, but the latter are not as hardy.

'Sundowner' produces spiky bronze-green leaves with pink or apricot margins

LAURUSTINUS *VIBURNUM TINUS*

HEIGHT AND SPREAD up to 8 × 8 ft (2.5 × 2.5 m)
SOIL Well-drained/moist but well-drained
HARDINESS Zones 7–9
SUN ☼ ☼

With its glossy, dark green oval leaves, this evergreen shrub is useful for year-round color on a roof terrace. It flowers in late winter, when heads of small, creamy-white flowers open from pink buds; these are followed by blue-black berries in summer. Happy in full sun or some shade and dry soil, this decorative shrub makes a good specimen for a large container or raised bed and offers a foil for brighter flowering plants. Remove overly long stems in late spring or early summer.

'Lucidum' is one of the largest laurustinus and can be trained to look like a small tree.

WINDOW DRESSING

Making a tiny garden on your windowsill for flowers, herbs, and even a few vegetables will enhance the look of your house or apartment while giving you a beautiful feature to enjoy from both indoors and outside. The strong sun and exposure on upper stories may dry out window displays quickly, so consider a self-watering trough or drought-tolerant plants if you don't have much time for maintenance. Safety also needs to be considered if your planters may pose a potential hazard if they fall.

Stone or lead troughs provide the perfect place for a dwarf agapanthus on the sill of a period home.

CHOOSING CONTAINERS

Lightweight troughs made from artificial materials or bamboo are the best options for upper-story windowsills because they will be easier to carry up and put in place once planted. Heavier stone, lead, and terra-cotta planters are suitable for ground-floor sills and can be more stable for large plants such as shrubs or perennials that may be top-heavy. In sun spots, a self-watering container that has an integrated reservoir at the base is a convenient option as it will keep plant roots moist for up to two weeks.

If you don't have a level, deep sill for a planter, measure the length of your trough and fix two heavy-duty metal hanging basket brackets on the wall beneath the window to support it. Choose traditional brackets with a level top edge and a curly hook at the end that will help keep the trough in place once it's in position (see below).

Hanging basket brackets can be secured below windows to support troughs where there are no sills.

Combine a small conifer, lemon thyme, pansies, grape hyacinths, and daffodils for a fall-to-spring display.

COLD-SEASON DISPLAYS

When deciding what to plant in your window boxes, opt for compact, drought-tolerant plants that can cope when confined to a small container. In fall and winter, choose from small or young evergreen shrubs, including little herbs such as thyme, as well as ferns, grasses, and violas and primulas in flower that will provide color during these darker days. You can also add a few bulbs such as grape hyacinths (*Muscari*), dwarf narcissi, or tiny tulips to extend the color into spring. To do this, add a layer of potting mix to the base of your trough, plant the bulbs and then set the other plants on top, filling in between their root balls with more potting mix. In spring, the bulbs will push their way through the gaps to create a bonanza of flowers and lush foliage.

SUMMER SPARKLERS

As the frosts recede, your choice of container plants expands to include the huge variety of tender bedding plants. If you used small shrubs in a winter display, you can replace these with summer blooms in late spring and replant the woody-stemmed plants in larger pots for the patio, if you have one, where they can put on more growth. Choose from the planting options on pp.96–99 for a long season of summer flowers, and remember to feed as well as water your plants when the fertilizer in the potting mix runs out in late summer—a high-potash feed is best for bedding. Keep deadheading flowers that need this treatment to extend your display into the fall. When colder weather returns, swap your plants around and start your cold-season collection off again—you may find that the little shrubs you replanted in patio pots to make way for summer flowers will still fit into the window box for another winter.

Other window box planting options include edibles such as lettuces (see p.106) or small houseplants, including tender succulents such as crassulas, echeverias, aeoniums, and paddle kalachoes, which should thrive on a windowsill tucked up close to the house where they won't get too cold or wet.

Vibrant pelargoniums matched with purple petunias, white bacopa, and pale yellow dwarf snapdragons make a sizzling summer display.

Tender succulents will enjoy the summer outside on a sill and can then be brought inside to decorate your home over winter.

Create a medley of small herbs for a scented edible windowsill that can remain in situ for a year or more.

HIGH-RISE RISKS

Choose a window box or trough that's just a little shorter than the length of your sill and not quite as wide, so that it will sit close to the window, where it's less likely to fall off. In areas prone to high winds and on narrow upper-story sills, install a grille to keep your flower displays in place and prevent accidents. Buy a metal grille that covers the whole window or a smaller one just deep enough to keep a trough in place.

Metal grilles will prevent pots and troughs from falling off upper-story windowsills and causing injury below.

PLANTS FOR WINDOWSILLS

Boxes and pots on windowsills can offer a confection of colorful plants to enjoy from both inside and outside your home, and many tender types will flower longer in the warmer conditions next to a house. This collection of bedding, ferns, and small bulbs can be augmented with young evergreen shrubs for winter displays, but most woody-stemmed plants will need to be repotted after a season or two as they start to grow. Consider also the smaller plants recommended for balconies (see pp.84–87), which will be equally happy on a windowsill.

SNAPDRAGON *ANTIRRHINUM*

HEIGHT AND SPREAD up to 24 × 24 in (60 × 60 cm)
POTTING MIX Peat-free
HARDINESS Zones 7–10
SUN ☼ ☼

These plants are loved for their spikes of hooded flowers that open like little jaws when pinched, hence their common name. Grow the larger varieties on the sills of tall windows that will allow you to look out over the top of them; dwarf bedding types (*Antirrhinum nanum*) are the best option for smaller apertures. The blooms come in a wide range of colors, and will appear from summer up to the first frosts, or beyond on a sheltered sill—they may even overwinter in mild areas.

The Liberty Classic Series bears colorful flowers, ideal for the sills of tall windows.

HART'S TONGUE FERN *ASPLENIUM SCOLOPENDRIUM*

HEIGHT AND SPREAD 16 × 16 in (40 × 40 cm)
POTTING MIX Peat-free with added topsoil
HARDINESS Zones 4–9
SUN ☼ ☼

If you're looking for inspiration for a shady windowsill or some winter color, try this compact evergreen fern. Its rosette of arching, glossy green fronds with wavy margins makes a beautiful leafy accompaniment to violas and spring bulbs, or combine it with other small ferns such as polypody (see p.86) for a cool green display. Keep the soil moist, particularly from spring to early fall when the fern is in full growth, and feed with an all-purpose granular fertilizer each spring, if it's in a pot year-on-year.

Wavy-edged lance-shaped evergreen leaves create year-round appeal on a sill.

SWAN RIVER DAISY *BRACHYSCOME IBERIDIFOLIA*

HEIGHT AND SPREAD 10 × 10 in (25 × 25 cm)
POTTING MIX Peat-free
HARDINESS Zones 3–11
SUN ☼

Drought-tolerance and a long flowering season make this Australian native ideal for a sunny sill, where its pretty daisy flowers will bloom all summer and fall, with little help from you. The finely divided foliage provides another decorative feature. Use it to trail over the sides of a window box instead of lobelia, which is prone to drying out halfway through the summer, and choose from shades of blue, mauve, pink, or white. Feed with a high-potash fertilizer if plants start to flag in late summer.

'Metallic Blue' has steely pale blue flowers that make a pretty edging for a window box.

MILLION BELLS *CALIBRACHOA*

HEIGHT AND SPREAD 10 × 12 in (25 × 30 cm)
POTTING MIX Peat-free
HARDINESS Zones 2–11
SUN ☼ ◐

The appropriately named million bells is a favorite for windowsills, offering trailing stems adorned with small bell-shaped flowers that look like tiny petunias. The huge color range offers something for everyone, from blue, purple, and red, to peach, pink, and white. The plants are self-cleaning, which means they will flower continuously throughout summer and early fall without deadheading. Keep potting mix moist and feed weekly with a high-potash fertilizer from late summer.

'Cabaret Lavender' produces cascading stems of rich purple flowers all summer.

FUCHSIA *FUCHSIA* (DWARF)

HEIGHT AND SPREAD Up to 20 × 20 in (50 × 50 cm)
POTTING MIX Peat-free
HARDINESS Zones 6–8
SUN ☼ ◐

Flowering in shady sites as well as in sun, fuchsias will dress up a windowsill display with their bright flowers, which dance on arching stems like tiny ballerinas. Choose a dwarf fuchsia for your box or pots, such as the upright 'Tom Thumb', 'Amy Lye', and 'Beacon', or the trailing 'Swingtime', 'Maori Maid', and 'Frosted Flame', which represent just a tiny selection of the thousands of plants on offer. Add a high-potash fertilizer every week or two in summer to keep them blooming.

'Frosted Flame' produces cascading stems of dainty white and dark pink flowers.

VERBENA *GLANDULARIA PERUVIANA*

HEIGHT AND SPREAD 10 × 10 in (25 × 25 cm)
POTTING MIX Peat-free
HARDINESS Zones 3–11
SUN ☼

Not to be confused with the tall garden plants, these bedding verbenas grow to just 10 in (25 cm) and have either an upright or trailing habit—check packaging information for the type you need. They require sun to put on a good display of red, white, purple, or pink flat-topped flowers, which appear in summer and early fall among toothed green leaves. Keep their potting mix moist and feed with a high-potash fertilizer from late summer. You may also find them listed as *Verbena peruviana*.

Verbenas come in a wide range of colors, including bi-colored forms, and they flower all summer.

CHERRY PIE *HELIOTROPIUM ARBORESCENS*

HEIGHT AND SPREAD up to 18 × 18 in (45 × 45 cm)
POTTING MIX Peat-free
HARDINESS Zones 3–11
SUN ☼ ◐

The scent of the violet-blue flowers of this shrubby plant is reminiscent of baked cherry pie, hence the name. Adding a cool note to brighter flowers in a windowsill display, the domed heads of small blooms appear all summer; flowering can be extended further if you deadhead regularly. Plants will also flower in part shade, but may produce fewer blooms. Try the very fragrant 'Reva', or 'Princess Marina' for a more compact plant. Apply a high-potash fertilizer weekly from late summer.

Cherry pie is a good choice for sunny sills, its flowers perfuming house interiors when the windows are open.

BUSY LIZZIE *IMPATIENS*

HEIGHT AND SPREAD 12 × 12 in (30 × 30 cm)
POTTING MIX Peat-free
HARDINESS Zones 2–11
SUN ☼ ☼

Renowned for their ability to bloom in the shade, these compact annuals will brighten up any windowsill with their colorful round flowers. They come in a rainbow of shades and bloom from early summer to the first frosts in the fall. The New Guinea Group are the largest type, with bigger flowers and dark foliage. Busy lizzies flower well for long periods without deadheading, but they do require moist potting mix and will wilt if it dries out. Apply a high-potash fertilizer weekly from late summer.

New Guinea busy lizzies are robust plants with round blooms and dark green foliage.

BROAD-LEAVED GRAPE HYACINTH

MUSCARI LATIFOLIUM

HEIGHT AND SPREAD 8 × 3 in (20 × 7.5 cm)
POTTING MIX Peat-free
HARDINESS Zones 3–9
SUN ☼ ☼

This beautiful grape hyacinth combines distinctive heads of dark blue-black spring flowers topped with a tuft of paler blue blooms and broad lance-shaped green leaves. Plant the bulbs in pots or a window box in the fall alongside small daffodils and violas for a breathtaking display the following spring. Keep the potting mix moist and leave the foliage to die down naturally, allowing flowers to reappear the following year.

The broad-leaved grape hyacinth produces compact bi-colored blooms for many weeks in spring.

SMALL DAFFODILS *NARCISSUS*

HEIGHT AND SPREAD up to 16 × 8 in (40 × 20 cm)
POTTING MIX Peat-free
HARDINESS Zones 3–8
SUN ☼ ☼

Dwarf daffodils usher in spring on a windowsill with their dainty nodding flowers and strappy green foliage. When selecting bulbs in the fall, opt for shorter varieties for a windowsill, such as the popular yellow-flowered 'Tête-à-tête', white 'Thalia', 'Hawera', with its flat lemon-colored blooms, and the sweetly scented jonquilla and tazetta narcissi. Plant the bulbs in the fall for a spring display and leave the foliage to die down naturally if you want flowers the following year.

'Thalia' has creamy-white flowers with swept-back petals, and blooms for several weeks.

NEMESIA *NEMESIA*

HEIGHT AND SPREAD 12 × 10 in (30 × 25 cm)
POTTING MIX Peat-free
HARDINESS Zones 2–11
SUN ☼ ☼

These floriferous annuals are decked with sprays of tiny, frilly-edged flowers from early summer to the first frosts, or longer on a sheltered windowsill. Many are sweetly scented, too, and the color range is vast, with something to suit every flower scheme. Their long flowering period and ability to bloom in a little shade makes them hard to beat, and they do not require deadheading. Keep the potting mix moist in summer and feed with a high-potash fertilizer from late summer.

The Lady Series of nemesias produce bi-colored, sweetly scented flowers.

WHITE LACE FLOWER *ORLAYA GRANDIFLORA*

HEIGHT AND SPREAD 24 × 18 in (60 × 45 cm)
POTTING MIX Peat-free
HARDINESS Zones 2–11
SUN ☼

White lace flower's dainty flat-topped flowers and ferny foliage have an airy look that lends a meadow-like style to a window box display. Blooming through summer and fall, the flowers also attract bees and butterflies. Mix lace flowers with other relaxed-looking blooms such as cherry pie and snapdragons to complete the look. They are drought-tolerant and able to cope with periods of neglect, but weekly feeds of a high-potash fertilizer from late summer will give them a boost if they start to flag.

The white lace flower's slim stems of white flowers appear through summer and fall.

AFRICAN DAISY *OSTEOSPERMUM*

HEIGHT AND SPREAD up to 18 × 18 in (45 × 45 cm)
POTTING MIX Peat-free
HARDINESS Zones 2–11
SUN ☼

Bedding types of African daisy are compact and their pretty blooms are available in colors ranging from white and yellow to pink and purple. The daisies appear from early summer until fall on slender stems above spoon-shaped green leaves. Plant sizes vary, so check labels for heights and spreads to ensure your choices suit your windowsill display. While not fully hardy, plants may survive the winter on a sill in a mild area. Feed plants with high-potash fertilizer in late summer.

The Serenity Series of African daisies are compact, free-flowering plants.

DUSTY MILLER *SENECIO CINERARIA*

HEIGHT AND SPREAD up to 16 × 12 in (40 × 30 cm)
POTTING MIX Peat-free
HARDINESS Zones 8–10
SUN ☼ ☀

A mainstay of container displays, the lacy silver foliage of dusty miller, also known as senecio, provides the perfect foil for flowering plants. It also produces clusters of daisylike yellow blooms, which can be removed if they don't suit your plans. Despite its exotic appearance and use in summer bedding displays, this little shrub is quite hardy and can also play a part in winter displays in mild areas, especially on a sill that offers protection from wet weather. Feed it with an all-purpose granular fertilizer in spring.

The silvery foliage of dusty miller provides a sparkling foil for brightly colored blooms.

VIOLA *VIOLA* HYBRIDS

HEIGHT AND SPREAD 8 × 6 in (20 × 15 cm)
POTTING MIX Peat-free
HARDINESS Zones 3–8
SUN ☼ ☀

Small-flowered violas make beautiful additions to a spring container display, their round flowers creating a riot of color alongside bulbs such as narcissi and grape hyacinths, or tucked between ferns. You will find violas in shades to suit almost any scheme and while they are often sold as winter bedding, unless you purchase them already in flower, they may not bloom until spring in cold areas. Also try trailing types such as the Endurio and Balconita Series to cascade over the sides of a planter.

Among the first flowers of spring, violas may bloom until the summer if deadheaded.

Many small herbs and vegetables
such as kohlrabi and celeriac can be grown
in containers to create a tiny productive
plot on a balcony or roof.

ADDING FEATURES
AND FURNISHINGS

Plot size need not limit your ambitions to grow your own
food. Small-scale fruits, vegetables, and herbs can be raised
on a windowsill or balcony, or you can create a productive
plot in a sunny spot with more ground space. A small space
also offers the perfect place to relax and unwind, with
lighting, sofas, and dining suites providing the best home
comforts outside. Check that the furniture you choose fits
the space comfortably and that you have somewhere to
store the cushions over winter.

MAKING A SMALL HERB GARDEN

Perfect for a small yard, balcony, or roof terrace, herbs are among the easiest edibles to grow. There are varieties for every site, including one in shade, and they grow well in free-draining soil in the ground, as well as in raised beds and pots. All herbs, including evergreens such as rosemary and sage, are dormant or grow very little in winter, so allow them to rest and do not pick the leaves at this time.

Bay trees can be trained to form lollipop-headed standards, which offer height and structure to an herb garden.

SITING HERBS

Many herbs hail from Mediterranean regions where they receive plenty of sun but little rain during the summer months. Their drought-resistance makes them perfect for growing in pots, raised beds, and free-draining soil, but many herbs will rot in heavy clay that's prone to waterlogging, particularly in winter, so grow them in a raised bed or container if you have this type of soil.

In shady gardens, choose parsley, mint, dill, chives, and oregano, which cope well with lower light levels. Cilantro is another option for a partly shaded site because, despite being a Mediterranean plant, it quickly goes to seed when grown in full sun—the seeds are edible but plants tend to die down after they have formed.

> **TOP TIP** WHEN HARVESTING LEAVES FROM HERBS, TAKE ONLY A FEW SPRIGS AT A TIME AND LEAVE ENOUGH FOLIAGE TO PHOTOSYNTHESIZE AND FEED THE PLANT, ALLOWING IT TO THRIVE.

Mint will thrive in some shade, but confine it to pots and planters if you don't want it to monopolize your beds.

Corten steel planters create a wall of herbs around a patio area, raising the plants to make harvesting easier.

An herb bed will need little extra irrigation once the plants are established, although annuals will require more regular watering.

CREATING AN HERB BED

If you have a free-draining soil and want a year-round, easy-care, scented feature, then a small herb garden will tick all your boxes. Offering evergreen foliage and spring and summer flowers, many of which are edible as well as attractive, herbs thrive when they are packed together in a bed. It is easy to make a traditional feature edged with Japanese holly (*Ilex crenata*) or a low hedge of dwarf lavender such as *Lavandula angustifolia* 'Little Lady'. Divide up the bed to accommodate a range of herbs, with taller plants such as bay, rosemary, and fennel in the center, sage; cilantro, and dill next in line; and low-growing thyme, parsley, oregano, marjoram, and basil providing an edging at the front. Do not plant mint in the bed, as it will swamp its neighbors.

SOWING ANNUALS

Many annual and biennial herbs such as basil and parsley are easy to grow from seed. In early spring, sow them in seed trays or small pots—recycled plastic or biodegradable containers are ideal—and place them on a sunny windowsill or in a heated greenhouse to germinate. Grow the seedling herbs on indoors, transplanting them into larger pots as their root systems expand. Plant them outside when the temperatures warm up in late spring—tender basil and cilantro should be kept inside until after the frosts have passed. Water plants in pots when the top of the potting mix feels dry and irrigate those in the ground during dry spells. The immature roots of annual herbs makes them more prone to drought stress, so they will need more water than mature perennials and shrubs grown in a bed.

EASY HERBS TO SOW FROM SEED:

Dill (*Anethum graveolens*) • Cilantro (*Coriandrum sativum*) • Bush or Greek basil (*Ocimum minimum*) • Parsley (*Petroselinum crispum*)

PLANTING IN POTS

Choose pots measuring about 8 in (20 cm) in diameter and height for annuals and larger containers for shrubby herbs, such as bay, rosemary, and sage, that you want to keep from year to year. Plant annuals in peat-free commercial potting mix; perennials and shrubs will prefer a 4:1 mix of peat-free potting mix with added topsoil and sand to ensure good drainage. When planting, take care not to bury the stems below the surface. Applying a layer of gravel, small pebbles, or other aggregates over the top of the potting mix after planting will help retain moisture and reduce weed growth. Raise your containers off the ground by setting them on pot feet or bricks, so that excess moisture can drain away. Water herbs in pots when the top of the soil feels dry.

A layer of slate chips covering the surface helps retain moisture in these small pots of thyme.

Sow herbs in trays or pots of seed starting mix and transplant to their own pots when they develop a few leaves.

PLANTS FOR HERB GARDENS

There are many different varieties of herb that will thrive in a container or border, but these represent some of the easiest edibles to grow in a small space. Mint and those that are vulnerable to frost are best confined to a container, while others, including thyme and oregano, can be left to wander between paving cracks or along the edges of a path or flowerbed. Add annuals such as cilantro, basil, and dill (see p.103), which you can grow from seed on a windowsill indoors if you have space, and plant out after the frosts.

LEMON VERBENA *ALOYSIA CITRODORA*

HEIGHT AND SPREAD up to 3¼ × 3¼ft (1 × 1 m)
SOIL Well-drained
HARDINESS Zones 9–11
SUN ☼

The narrow lemon-scented leaves of this shrubby deciduous herb are produced in abundance from summer to early fall and make a soothing tea. Sprays of tiny white or pale lilac flowers also appear in summer. Grow lemon verbena in a pot in a sunny site, and move it to a sheltered spot or protect it with layers of fleece in winter; keeping the potting mix dry by placing it close to the house will also help protect it. Feed annually in spring with half the recommended dose of an all-purpose granular fertilizer.

Lemon verbena is not fully hardy but will cope with the cold better if its soil is dry.

CHIVES *ALLIUM SCHOENOPRASUM*

HEIGHT AND SPREAD up to 12 × 12 in (30 × 30 cm)
SOIL Well-drained/moist but well-drained
HARDINESS Zones 3–9
SUN ☼ ☼

The slim hollow stems and leaves of this perennial herb add a delicate onion flavor to savory dishes and salads. It is easy to grow and tolerant of some shade. Plant it in a pot or border, where it will provide fresh green stems and leaves throughout summer and early fall, after which it dies down over winter; new growth will reappear the following spring. Pink pompom flowers appear in summer and are also edible. Apply half the recommended dose of all-purpose granular fertilizer to potted plants in spring.

Chives are very easy to grow in pots or a border and can be harvested over many months.

MINT *MENTHA*

HEIGHT AND SPREAD up to 30 × 30 in (75 × 75 cm)
SOIL Well-drained
HARDINESS Zones 3–8
SUN ☼ ☼

There are many types of mint to choose from, ranging from green-leaved spearmint (*Mentha spicata*) to the variegated, fruit-scented leaves of pineapple mint (*Mentha suaveolens* 'Variegata') and the dark green foliage of chocolate peppermint (*Mentha* × *piperita* f. *citrata* 'Chocolate'). One trait they all share is their vigorous, spreading habit—they will soon smother their neighbors if grown in a bed, so restrain them in a pot. Feed with an all-purpose granular fertilizer in spring.

Pineapple mint is just one of the many flavored varieties you can grow in a pot.

OREGANO *ORIGANUM VULGARE*

HEIGHT AND SPREAD 12 × 24 in (30 × 60 cm)
SOIL Well-drained
HARDINESS Zones 5–12
SUN ☼ ☀

This easy-going perennial herb will spread to form a leafy, edible carpet around a patio or along the edges of a flowerbed, or grow it in a pot. Its aromatic small leaves and small pollen-rich pink summer flowers make a decorative feature, as well as enriching the flavor of many savory dishes. Oregano is also useful for shady spots, growing well where other herbs would struggle. In spring, prune out old stems, and add half the recommended dose of all-purpose granular fertilizer to potted plants.

Oregano will form a frilly edge to a bed of herbs or can be grown in a pot.

COMMON SAGE *SALVIA OFFICINALIS*

HEIGHT AND SPREAD to 30 × 30 in (75 × 75 cm)
SOIL Well-drained
HARDINESS Zones 4–11
SUN ☼ ☀

The rough-textured gray-green leaves of this evergreen sub-shrub are joined by pale blue flowers in early summer, and both can be used to flavor a wide range of dishes. Other choices include the purple-leaved 'Purpurascens' and 'Tricolor', a pretty variegated form. Sage grows well in pots when young but this sprawling plant often performs better when planted in the ground as it matures. In spring, cut back old growth and feed potted sages with an all-purpose granular fertilizer.

'Tricolor' is a decorative sage, with variegated green, cream, and purple-flushed edible foliage.

ROSEMARY *SALVIA ROSMARINUS*

HEIGHT AND SPREAD up to 5 × 5 ft (1.5 × 1.5 m)
SOIL Well-drained
HARDINESS Zones 7–10
SUN ☼

Tall, shrubby rosemary is a great choice for a border or raised bed, where it will bear its needlelike leaves all year round—but do not pick them in winter when it's dormant as this will weaken the plant. Another option is trailing rosemary (*Salvia rosmarinus* Prostratus Group), which will spill over the sides of a large pot or create a green edging for a border. Both produce small purple-blue edible flowers from spring to early summer. Feed potted plants in spring with an all-purpose granular fertilizer.

Trailing rosemary makes a good edging plant for a large container or raised bed.

THYME *THYMUS*

HEIGHT AND SPREAD 6 × 20 in (15 × 50 cm)
SOIL Well-drained
HARDINESS Zones 5–9
SUN ☼

Plant this little herb at the edge of a large pot or grow it in a bed, harvesting its small oval leaves from spring to early fall. Choose from common thyme (*Thymus vulgaris*), lemon-scented thyme (*Thymus* × *citriodorus*), or the large thyme (*Thymus pulegioides*), which grows a little taller than its relatives. Edible white or pink flowers also appear in summer. Feed potted plants with half the recommended dose of all-purpose granular fertilizer in spring.

'Golden King' is a variegated thyme with gold-edged green leaves and pink summer flowers.

CREATING A TINY VEGETABLE PLOT

Biting into a ripe tomato or savoring a spicy radish that you've grown yourself is one of life's great pleasures, and you can create an edible plot for these and other vegetables in the tiniest of spaces. From a window box filled with salad leaves to a raised bed packed with produce, small spaces offer plenty of scope, while sowing seed will broaden your crop choices and allow you to experiment with new flavors.

Ideal for balconies, this unit holds three trays for small crops; turn the trays every day to expose all the plants to the sun.

WHAT AND WHERE TO GROW VEGETABLES

Your ambitions to grow vegetables need not be restricted by the size of your available space, whether it is on a patio, up on a roof or balcony, or in a bed in the yard. The light in your garden is a consideration, however, and many crops such as tomatoes, peppers, and onions demand a sunny spot, while others, including salad leaves, beets, chard, kale, and kohlrabi, will thrive in light shade. Few crops succeed in deep shade, so choose the brightest spot you have available for the best results.

A small vegetable plot in a raised bed in the yard or on a patio offers the space to grow a wide selection of edibles. Many vegetable crops also thrive in containers, as long as they are deep enough for the developing root systems to expand. You will have to water and possibly feed crops in pots regularly, too, especially those that will be basking in hot sun, which will quickly dry out the potting mix. Consider installing an automatic watering system to guarantee a good harvest (see p.128) if you are unable to water every day or two during the spring and summer months.

Grow the vegetables you most enjoy and, if you're feeling adventurous, experiment with new varieties that are only available in seed form to home growers. Plant different types of vegetable in the soil each year to avoid a buildup of crop-specific pests and diseases, such as potato and tomato blight. Where space is tight, you can alternate growing areas, planting your favorite crops in the ground and then in pots for a few years before planting in the soil again. Clean the pots each year, too.

Woven willow hurdles create a small raised bed packed with sweet corn, zucchini, and edible nasturtium flowers.

Lettuce seeds can be sown directly into pots and the leaves cut when 6in (15cm) high; the stubs then produce a new crop.

SOILS AND POTTING MIXES

Before sowing seed or planting young crops, prepare your bed well. In the fall before a spring planting, remove stones, debris, and large pernicious weeds from the soil surface, and cover it with a layer of cardboard, or about six sheets of newspaper. Then add a 2-in (5-cm) layer of well-rotted organic compost (see p.17) over the cardboard or paper. This cuts out the sunlight and will kill most of the remaining weeds, while helping prevent new ones from germinating. The cardboard and organic matter will also rot down over winter, helping improve the soil structure and creating moist, fertile conditions for your crops. Before planting, remove any weeds that have managed to survive.

When growing in pots, use peat-free potting mix for your annual crops. Scrub the pots with hot water and detergent and change the potting mix each year to avoid passing on pests and diseases to the next season's crops.

In the fall, cover the soil with layers of cardboard and organic compost to improve the soil, ready for a spring planting.

HOW TO SOW SEEDS INDOORS

You can buy young vegetable plants in spring, but there is a greater choice of varieties available as seed. Follow these steps to sow tender types such as tomatoes, peppers, and zucchini, and hardy crops that are vulnerable to slug damage—keeping seedlings protected until they are larger plants gives them a greater chance of survival.

YOU WILL NEED Small pots or cell trays • Peat-free seed starting mix • Seeds • Vermiculite (optional) • Recycled plant pots • Peat-free potting mix

1 Fill small pots or cells with peat-free seed starting mix and gently press it down to remove any large air gaps. Sow 2–3 seeds per pot or 1–2 per cell. Chile seeds are shown here.
2 Check seed packs for sowing depths and cover the seeds accordingly. Tiny seeds need light to germinate, so sprinkle just enough potting mix or vermiculite (a water-absorbent mineral that allows light to penetrate to the seeds) over them; larger seeds will need to be buried deeper. Water gently.

3 Place the seed pots or trays on a bright windowsill out of direct sun. Keep the potting mix moist, but guard against waterlogging. Seedlings should appear within 2–3 weeks.
4 When the seedlings have a few sets of leaves, gently lift them out of their containers by holding the leaves and using a teaspoon to scoop out the roots. Repot each seedling in a small pot of its own to grow on. When the plant has filled that container, plant in the soil or in containers outside after the frosts have passed.

VEGETABLES FOR SMALL SPACES

If you're tempted to grow a few vegetables in your small space, try these for starters. All are easy to grow and many thrive in pots of peat-free growing mix with added fertilizer. Planting a range of containers with different vegetables will help maximize your productivity and ensure that if one succumbs to crop-specific disease, you won't lose the lot. Avoid growing tomatoes and potatoes close together, however, as both are at risk from blight; choose early-cropping varieties, too, since the disease often attacks plants later in the summer.

SPRING ONIONS *ALLIUM FISTULOSUM*

HEIGHT AND SPREAD up to 12 × 2 in (30 × 5 cm)
SOIL Well-drained
SOW Spring through fall
SUN ☼ ☼

Perfect for pots, these little onions are quick and easy to grow. Either buy young seedlings or sow seed in pots of peat-free potting mix. Alternatively, sow in the soil 4 in (10 cm) apart. Sow small quantities every two weeks from spring to fall for a long harvest. Do not thin seedlings; leave them to grow closely together and harvest the onions before they get too congested. Water during dry spells. Harvest the onions about 8 weeks after sowing, when plants are 6–8 in (15–20 cm) tall.

Spring onions sown in pots or the soil will be ready to harvest after about two months.

ONIONS *ALLIUM CEPA*

HEIGHT AND SPREAD up to 30 × 24 in (75 × 60 cm)
SOIL Well-drained
SOW Spring or fall, depending on type
SUN ☼

Grow onions from sets (small onion bulbs) in beds in spring after mulching the soil in the fall with organic compost (*see p.107*). Plant them 2–4 in (5–10 cm) apart, with 10 in (25 cm) between rows, with the pointed ends just showing above the surface. Cover with fleece to prevent bird damage until your crops are established. Water the soil around the sets every 14 days during dry weather until midsummer; try to avoid wetting the plants. Lift bulbs from late summer when the foliage turns yellow but before it dies down.

Harvest onions on a sunny day and leave the bulbs to dry off on the soil before storing.

SWISS CHARD

BETA VULGARIS SUBSP. *CICLA* VAR. *FLAVESCENS*

HEIGHT AND SPREAD 18 × 18 in (45 × 45 cm)
SOIL Well-drained
SOW Spring, fall to overwinter
SUN ☼ ☼

The colorful stems and dark green leaves of Swiss chard can be harvested from midsummer to winter and eaten raw or steamed. In spring, buy seedlings or sow seed thinly into shallow drills about ¾ in (2 cm) deep and 12 in (30 cm) apart, then cover with soil and water. You can also sow the seed thinly in large pots of peat-free potting mix. If seeds produce more than one seedling, thin to leave one plant to mature. Water well.

The colorful leafy stems of Swiss chard can be harvested throughout fall and winter.

BEETS *BETA VULGARIS SUBSP. VULGARIS*

HEIGHT AND SPREAD 12 × 8 in (30 × 20 cm)
SOIL Well-drained
SOW Spring through late summer
SUN ☼ ☼

Easy to grow in pots of peat-free potting mix or in a small raised bed, these little purple nutrient bombs are delicious and packed with vitamins. In mid-spring, sow 2–3 seeds in one spot in holes 1 in (2.5 cm) deep and 4 in (10 cm) apart. After germination, remove the weakest seedling and add it to salads. Sow small batches every two weeks until late summer for a long harvest. Water your plants regularly and pull the roots when they're about the size of a golf ball—larger roots can often taste woody.

The cylindrical roots of beet 'Alto' can be packed into pots on a balcony or roof.

KOHLRABI *BRASSICA OLERACEA* (GONGYLODES GROUP)

HEIGHT AND SPREAD 18 × 18 in (45 × 45 cm)
SOIL Moist but well-drained
SOW Spring or fall
SUN ☼ ☼

Rarely seen in the shops, these sweet little cabbage-like swollen stems can be grown in pots and small beds. Sow seed directly into a prepared bed or pot of peat-free potting mix and when seedlings are about 1 in (2.5 cm) tall, thin to a final spacing of 6–8 in (15–20 cm). Sow seed in batches from spring to summer for a long harvest. Water during dry spells and cover plants with fleece to prevent attacks from birds and cabbage root fly. Harvest when the crops are the size of a golf or tennis ball.

Purple kohlrabi looks as good as it tastes and grows well in large containers.

MIZUNA *BRASSICA RAPA* SSP. *NIPPOSINICA*

HEIGHT AND SPREAD up to 10 × 10 in (25 × 25 cm)
SOIL Moist but well-drained
SOW Fall
SUN ☼ ☼

Often paired with mibuna in a seed pack, mizuna is a quick and easy leafy crop for salads and stir-fries. In early spring, sow seed thinly in rows in a prepared bed or large container filled with peat-free potting mix, and thin the seedlings to 6–8 in (15–20 cm) apart. Sow in batches every few weeks from spring to midsummer for a long harvest of leaves. Keep plants well watered to prevent them flowering (known as "bolting"). If slugs are a problem, grow mizuna in pots on a windowsill out of harm's way.

Mizuna adds a spicy note to salads and stir-fries, and crops from summer to fall.

CHILE PEPPER *CAPSICUM FRUTESCENS*

HEIGHT AND SPREAD 24 × 20 in (60 × 50 cm)
SOIL Moist but free-draining
SOW Spring only
SUN ☼

These hot and spicy fruiting vegetables can be grown from seed, or you can buy young plants in spring. To sow seed, follow the steps on p.107. When the plants have a few strong stems, nip out the tips with your fingers or sharp pruners, which will produce bushier plants with more fruits. Set plants outside after the frosts have passed in a sunny, sheltered area, when daytime temperatures are consistently above 61°F (16°C). Keep plants well watered, and use a cane to support tall, fruiting stems.

The fruits of the hot chile 'Tabasco' turn from yellow to bright red as they ripen.

ZUCCHINI *CUCURBITA PEPO*

HEIGHT AND SPREAD 32 × 32 in (80 × 80 cm)
SOIL Moist but well-drained
SOW Warm season only
SUN ☼

Zucchini is easy to sow from seed and the resulting plants, while quite large, will be happy in containers on a sunny patio. In late spring, sow two seeds in a small pot of seed starting mix and keep them on a bright windowsill (see p.107). Remove the weakest seedling when both have a few leaves. Grow on indoors until all risk of frost has passed, then plant each zucchini in a large pot of peat-free potting mix or in beds 3 ft (90 cm) apart. Avoid wetting the leaves to prevent mildew.

Tuck dry straw under the zucchini flowers and fruits to prevent them from rotting.

CARROT *DAUCUS CAROTA*

HEIGHT AND SPREAD up to 12 × 6 in (30 × 15 cm)
SOIL Moist but well-drained
SOW Spring through fall
SUN ☼

Carrots are easy to grow, but for success, guard against carrot fly and choose a pest-resistant variety. In mid-spring, sow seed thinly outside, ½ in (1 cm) deep and in rows 6 in (15 cm) apart, either in the soil or in a large planter filled with peat-free potting mix. Cover with fine netting to prevent the carrot fly laying its eggs close to your crops. Thin seedlings to 2 in (5 cm) apart, and sow batches every 3–4 weeks for a long harvest. Water during dry spells, and pick when roots are pushing out of the soil.

Planting carrots in tall pots can protect crops from attack by the low-flying carrot fly.

LETTUCE *LACTUCA SATIVA*

HEIGHT AND SPREAD up to 10 × 10 in (25 × 25 cm)
SOIL Moist but free-draining
SOW Spring or fall, dislikes heat
SUN ☼ ☀

Lettuce is a reliable and easy crop if you can protect the seedlings from slugs and snails by growing your crops in a window box or pot raised off the ground. From mid-spring, sow seed in shallow drills, cover with potting mix and either leave the seedlings to grow on if you plan to use them as cut-and-come-again leaves (see p.106) or thin to 6 in (15 cm) apart to allow plants to develop larger heads. An even easier option is to plant up seedlings from a garden center or supermarket. Keep plants well watered.

Mixed lettuces, mustard leaves, and pot marigolds create a beautiful edible display.

SNOW PEAS *PISUM SATIVUM* VAR. *SACCHARATUM*

HEIGHT AND SPREAD up to 36 × 12 in (90 × 30 cm)
SOIL Moist but well-drained
SOW Spring or fall
SUN ☼

Snow and sugar snap peas are the edible pods of immature peas, which can be steamed, boiled, or eaten raw. In late spring, make a flat-bottomed trench 2 in (5 cm) deep and 6 in (15 cm) wide and sow the seeds into it 3 in (7.5 cm) apart, then cover with soil and add fleece to deter pigeons. Push in twiggy shrub prunings or attach netting to bamboo canes for their scrambling stems to climb up. Keep plants well watered, and pick the pods regularly to encourage more to form.

The crisp green snow pea pods that emerge in summer are an easy-to-grow crop.

RADISH *RAPHANUS SATIVUS*

HEIGHT AND SPREAD 6 × 4 in (15 × 10 cm)
SOIL Moist but well-drained
SOW Spring or fall, dislikes heat
SUN ☼ ◑

One of the quickest crops to mature, radishes grow well in the soil or pots of peat-free potting mix. In spring, sow the seed of these crunchy roots 1 in (2.5 cm) apart in shallow drills, then cover and water in gently. Sow every few weeks for a long succession of crops. Keep plants moist at all times to prevent them flowering (bolting), which makes the radishes taste woody. Apply a seaweed feed once the plants are growing well. The roots should be ready for harvesting 4–6 weeks after sowing.

Radishes are easy to grow and can be harvested just a few weeks after sowing the seeds.

TOMATO *SOLANUM LYCOPERSICUM*

HEIGHT AND SPREAD up to 6½ × 1¾ ft (2 × 0.5 m)
SOIL Moist but free-draining
SOW Spring, needs warmth
SUN ☼

Choose bushy trailing tomatoes for hanging baskets or disease-resistant outdoor indeterminate varieties, which fruit on the side-shoots of a tall main stem, for large pots or a prepared bed in the garden or on a terrace. Sow seed indoors in mid-spring (see p.107) or buy young plants in late spring and plant outside after the frosts in a sheltered sunny spot. Stake indeterminate plants or use tomato cages. Feed about every 2 weeks. Water tomatoes consistently in order to prevent split fruits.

The cascading stems of an outdoor trailing cherry tomato produce heavy crops of fruit.

POTATOES *SOLANUM TUBEROSUM*

HEIGHT AND SPREAD up to 30 × 24 in (75 × 60 cm)
SOIL Moist but free-draining
SOW Spring only
SUN ☼

Potatoes can be grown in a trash can or tall growing bag with drainage holes in the base. In early spring, stand seed potatoes in an egg carton with the dents facing up and set on a windowsill indoors to sprout shoots. When the shoots are 1¼ in (3 cm) long, rub off all but four per tuber. Place 2–3 tubers on 8 in (20 cm) of peat-free potting mix and cover with 4 in (10 cm) of potting mix. Keep covering the stems as they grow until the container is full. Leave to grow on and harvest in summer.

Plant tubers in the bottom of a trash can, and cover the stems with soil until it's full.

SWEET CORN *ZEA MAYS*

HEIGHT AND SPREAD up to 5 × 1¾ ft (1.5 × 0.5 m)
SOIL Moist but well-drained
SOW Spring to summer, requires heat
SUN ☼

These tall, slim vegetables allow planting faster-maturing crops like radishes between them, maximizing your use of a small space. In late spring, sow seed indoors (see p.107) and keep on a windowsill until after the frosts. Then plant seedlings outside in a sunny, sheltered spot about 18 in (45 cm) apart in a block, which aids wind pollination. Water plants during dry spells. Feed every 2 weeks with a high nitrogen feed. Harvest when the silky tassels turn brown and the kernels release a milky liquid when pressed.

Harvest sweet corn when the silky tassels are brown and kernels release a milky liquid.

TINY FRUIT GARDENS

Fruit plants, bushes, and trees will all fit into tiny spaces if you choose your plants carefully. Strawberries will thrive in a planter on a windowsill or balcony, while dwarf fruit trees bred for growing in containers or small yards offer a wide choice of delicious flavors—though you must water those in pots regularly to guarantee their survival. Walls and fences also provide props for fruits such as blackberries, which can be trained along horizontal wires, or you can use your vertical surfaces to create sun traps for heat-loving fruits such as oranges and lemons (see *also pp.114–115*).

Dwarf apple trees will produce a good crop when grown in large pots on a sunny balcony, if you water them regularly.

FRUIT OPTIONS

Planting strawberries in a pot is one of the easiest ways to grow fruit if you're new to gardening, since these compact plants rarely disappoint if you water them regularly. Thornless blackberries are another easy option, but they need space in the ground or in a large planter to accommodate their roots, plus wires or trellis affixed to a wall or fence to create a framework for their sprawling stems—tie new growth into the supports regularly in spring. White currants, red currants, gooseberries, and rhubarb can also be grown in a bed or a large pot of peat-free potting mix with fertilizer, while blueberries will thrive in containers of lime-free potting mix (see *also p.115*).

While most fruits need sun to ripen, many plants can produce a good crop in part shade if they receive a few hours of direct sun each day. Blackberries and rhubarb are the most shade-tolerant, but even these will not be happy in a dark spot under a tree.

Strawberry plants are very easy to grow in pots on a sunny or partly shaded patio, balcony, or roof terrace.

GROWING CITRUS TREES

More adventurous gardeners may wish to try a few citrus plants, such as lemons and oranges, in their yard or on a patio, balcony, or roof terrace. Plant them in large containers with drainage holes, filled with a 4:1 mix of soil-based potting mix and sharp washed sand. After the frosts, set them outside in full sun. Citrus plants need plenty of water during the spring and summer—they prefer rainwater, if you have a rain barrel.

These are not hardy plants and they will need to come under cover for the winter, when they require cool but frost-free conditions—centrally heated homes are too warm. A heated greenhouse, cool conservatory, or unheated but bright room indoors will offer suitable accommodation for them during the cold seasons. In late spring, remove the top 2 in (5 cm) of old potting mix and replace it with fresh potting mix. Apply specialized summer and winter citrus fertilizers accordingly throughout the year, as instructed on the packaging.

Orange trees grow well in pots outside in summer but need a minimum winter temperature of 45°F (7°C).

DWARF FRUIT TREE GUIDE

If you would like a small fruit tree, first consider what size will suit your space best. Trees are grafted on to rootstocks that control their height and vigor (*see right*); for example, a dwarfing rootstock will produce a small tree that bears a good crop of fruit. You can also buy trees that produce two varieties of the same fruit, such as an apple or pear, on one tree, giving you two flavors for the price of one.

Check if the tree you want is self-fertile or needs a pollination partner, which means that you will require two trees for fruit to form. So, on a balcony with limited space, opt for a self-fertile type. Trees with disease-resistance are also worth seeking out.

The apple **'Winter Gem'** has been grafted on to a M27 dwarfing rootstock to produce a tiny tree that bears sweet eating apples in the fall.

DWARFING ROOTSTOCKS FOR TINY TREES

Reputable fruit tree nurseries usually offer a range of rootstocks for each variety that produce trees of different sizes, as outlined below.

APPLES
Rootstock: M27 (extremely dwarfing)
Suitable for: Small yards, containers
Starts fruiting: After 2 years
Height & spread: 4–6 ft (1.2–1.8 m) x 5 ft (1.5 m)

Rootstock: M9 (dwarfing)
Suitable for: Small yards, containers
Start fruiting: After 2–3 years
Height & spread: 6–8 ft (1.8–2.5 m) x 9 ft (2.7 m)

Rootstock: M26 (dwarfing)
Suitable for: Small yards, containers
Starts fruiting: After 2–3 years
Height & spread: 8–10 ft (2.5–3 m) x 12 ft (3.6 m)

PEARS AND QUINCES
Rootstock: Quince C (dwarfing)
Suitable for: Small yards, containers
Starts fruiting: After 4 years
Height & spread: 8–10 ft (2.5–3 m) x 8 ft (2.5 m)

Rootstock: Quince A (semi-vigorous)
Suitable for: Small yards
Starts fruiting: After 4 years
Height & spread: 10–15 ft (3–4.5 m) x 10 ft (3 m)

PLUMS AND DAMSONS
Rootstock: Pixy (semi-dwarfing)
Suitable for: Small yards, containers
Starts fruiting: After 3–4 years
Height & spread: 6–8 ft (1.8–2.5 m) x 6 ft (1.8 m)

CHERRY
Rootstock: Gisela 5 (semi-dwarfing)
Suitable for: Small yards, containers
Starts fruiting: After 3–4 years
Height & spread: 6–8 ft (1.8–2.5 m) x 6 ft (1.8 m)

A pear tree grafted on a Quince C rootstock will produce a good crop when grown in a large pot or in the ground.

FRUIT FOR A SMALL PLOT

Soft fruits such as strawberries, blueberries, and red currants are compact and easy-to-grow plants, suitable for a small balcony or up on a roof. If you have a little more space, a blackberry can be trained on the wall or fence of a patio or small yard, and it's a good choice for a shady space. Keep potted plants well watered during the growing season, as poor or intermittent moisture can affect the development of the fruit, causing a poor crop. Regular feeding will help produce a rich harvest, especially if your fruits are growing in containers.

BLACKBERRY *RUBUS FRUTICOSUS*

HEIGHT AND SPREAD 6½ × 6½ ft (2 × 2 m)
SOIL Well-drained/moist but well-drained
HARDINESS Zones 3–10
SUN ☼ ☼

Choose a thornless blackberry such as 'Loch Ness' or 'Loch Maree' and grow these bountiful plants in the ground or a raised bed. The long stems can be trained along wires or a large trellis in a small yard or on a terrace. New plants may not fruit until the summer after planting because they crop on stems produced the previous year. Keep blackberries well watered until established, and feed annually in spring with an all-purpose granular fertilizer, adding an organic mulch (see p.17) at the same time.

'Loch Maree' is a thornless blackberry that produces double pink flowers and sweet berries.

RED CURRANT *RIBES RUBRUM*

HEIGHT AND SPREAD up to 5 × 5 ft (1.5 × 1.5 m)
SOIL Well-drained/moist but well-drained
HARDINESS Zones 3–7
SUN ☼ ☼

These jewel-like berries grow well in the ground or in large pots, producing a crop of summer fruits on long, scrambling stems. Train them along wires fixed to a fence or wall or up a tripod of canes in a large pot. They are easy to grow—just feed them with a high-potash granular fertilizer in early spring, adding a mulch of organic matter (see p.17) at the same time. If growing plants in pots, apply a liquid fertilizer every fortnight from late winter to early spring, and an all-purpose granular fertilizer in spring.

'Jonkheer van Tets' will produce a heavy summer crop of tart-flavored currants.

BLUEBERRY *VACCINIUM CORYMBOSUM*

HEIGHT AND SPREAD 3¼ × 3¼ ft (1 × 1 m)
SOIL Moist but well-drained; acidic
HARDINESS Zones 3–7
SUN ☼ ☼

Blueberries are a popular fruiting crop for pots. Two plants are generally needed to produce a good harvest, although a few cultivars are self-fertile if you only have space for one—the best is 'Sunshine Blue'. The sweet fruits appear in late summer or early fall. Blueberries need acid soil (see p.16) to thrive, so grow them in large pots of lime free potting mix if your garden does not offer suitable conditions. Keep the potting mix moist and feed from spring to fall with a liquid fertilizer for acid-loving plants.

'Bluetta' is a compact blueberry that produces its early fruits from midsummer.

STRAWBERRY *FRAGARIA*

The taste of summer, sweet, fragrant strawberries are among the easiest fruits to grow in a small space. Plant them in containers, in hanging baskets, or in the ground and choose a selection of different varieties for berries all summer. The fruits fall into the following three groups.

HEIGHT AND SPREAD Up to 12 x 12 in (30 x 30 cm)
SOIL Moist but well-drained
HARDINESS Zones 5–8
SUN ☀ ◑

'Elsanta' is an early-season strawberry that produces large orange-red fruits.

JUNE-BEARING

For the largest fruits, choose June-bearing varieties. Divided into three groups, they include early-season plants that fruit in early summer; mid-season fruiters that crop in midsummer; and late varieties, which will provide you with berries a little later in summer. If you have space, try all three for a long harvest. These plants all crop well when grown in large pots of potting mix with topsoil, or plant them in the soil and tuck some straw beneath the developing fruits to prevent them rotting on the ground. They fruit best in their second and third years and throw out runners (stems with baby plantlets at the end) that will make new plants.

EVERBEARING

Also known as remontant or perpetual strawberries, these produce a continuous supply of sweet fruits throughout the summer and fall. They are a good choice if you want a small number of berries over a long period, and will fruit up to the first frosts. Everbearers also produce a good crop later in the season in their first year. A recent innovation is the climbing everbearer, which carries its fruits on tall stems up to 3¼ft (1 m) in length that can be trained up canes or on a trellis. Like June-bearing varieties, everbearers send out baby plantlets on runners that can be used to produce new plants.

'Toscana' produces pretty pink flowers followed by large, sweet fruits from summer until autumn.

ALPINE

These little shade-loving plants are also known as wild or woodland strawberries and can be grown in pots or between other plants in a border. They produce a succession of small, sweet fruits from midsummer to early fall. The plants are disease-resistant and the berries rarely rot since they're held above the soil. Alpines require very little care and are more drought-tolerant than the larger berries, requiring less frequent irrigation when grown in pots, making them a good choice for the time-poor gardener. Alpines reproduce via seed rather than runners and, where happy, they will spread year after year.

Alpines produce small, sweet fruits from summer to early fall on compact, disease-resistant plants.

INTRODUCING WATER

The sight and sound of a water feature will bring any small space to life. Most balconies, roofs, and patios can accommodate a containerized pool or a plug-in fountain, which will throw spangles of sunlight into your space and introduce soothing sounds to help you relax. The wildlife will appreciate a drink from your feature, too, as long as no chemicals are used to keep the water clear. Small water features are easy to care for, but be prepared to top them up in summer and to remove weeds from ponds.

This tiny Japanese-style garden features a traditional shishi-odoshi bamboo water spout with basin.

Still, reflective water adds a sense of calm to a small space and the aquatic plants increase its biodiversity.

WHY INCLUDE WATER?

Introducing a water feature offers many benefits, both to you and to wildlife. Reflective water adds a sense of calm and brings more light into your space, while small fountains and tiny cascades animate a space with relaxing sounds and movement. Insects, including bees, and other small creatures will be drawn to water features to quench their thirst, while birds will also use the water to loosen dirt from their feathers and keep them in good condition. A barrel pool may tempt frogs and toads to make a home there, if the water is at least 2 ft (60 cm) deep and the potted plants (see *opposite*) offer them jumping boards to access the pool easily and provide some camouflage.

TINY WATER FEATURES

There are many different water features available, so choose one to suit your space and style. Stylish water blades, where water pours from a letterbox-style opening into a reservoir below, suit contemporary designs, while a small pond or pool made from a watertight half barrel would fit perfectly into an informal wildlife garden. Lightweight, plug-in fountain features take up little space on balconies and roof terraces, and a bubbling urn will introduce an elegant sculptural feature to a patio garden. You will need an outdoor electricity supply, installed by a qualified electrician, for a fountain or cascade, or you can opt for a solar-powered feature if you have a sunny spot to install the charger.

This barrel pool is home to miniature cattails and waterlilies, together with frogs during the spring breeding season.

Water blades make eye-catching focal points while taking up very little space.

MAKE SPACE FOR PLANTS

Plants adapted to life in and around a pond offer a colorful palette that will extend your range, but take care when making your selections, since some vigorous aquatics will quickly outgrow

A dwarf water lily, an iris, and a spike rush (*Eleocharis palustris*) work well in a watertight glazed pot.

a small space (see pp.118–119 for recommendations). Most water plants prefer full sun or part shade, but few enjoy deep shade, so install your feature where they will thrive. Be prepared to fish out duckweed (little round floating leaves) and algae from time to time to keep the water clear. You can buy eco-friendly products that help minimize weed growth, but check that they will not affect other plants, too.

HOW TO PLANT AN AQUATIC

Constrain your water plants in planting baskets or bags to keep their growth in check, following the simple steps below. Check plant labels for their preferred planting depths (*see below*) and set them at the correct levels in your pool.

YOU WILL NEED Water plant • Trowel • Aquatic potting soil • Pond plant basket or bag • Washed gravel

1   Store your water plant in a shallow pan of water in part shade when you bring it home. When you are ready to plant it, add a thin layer of aquatic potting soil to the base of the pond basket or bag. Tip the plant out of its original container and place it on top of the soil.
2   Add soil around the edge of the root ball until the basket or bag is full. Check that the plant stems are not submerged beneath the soil and firm it gently with your hands to remove any air gaps.
3   Apply a layer of washed gravel over the surface of the soil to help prevent it from muddying the water. Gently firm down the gravel.
4   Place the plant into your water feature at the correct pond depth— this is the measurement from the top of the basket to the water surface. If the pool is too deep, set your plant basket on bricks or stones to raise it.

1

2

3

4

TOP TIP KEEP YOUR POND OR WATER FEATURE TOPPED UP DURING HOT SPELLS. USE RAINWATER FROM A BARREL, OR LEAVE TAP WATER IN A BUCKET FOR A DAY OR TWO TO ALLOW THE CHLORINE TO DISSIPATE BEFORE ADDING IT. USE A KITCHEN STRAINER TO LIFT OUT DUCKWEED AND REMOVE ALGAE BY TWIRLING IT AROUND A STICK.

PLANTS FOR TINY PONDS

Small ponds offer a great opportunity to expand your planting palette, with dwarf water lilies and compact perennials creating a tapestry of colors and textures above the reflective surface. Choose carefully, however, as some vigorous aquatic plants that may look small when you buy them can swamp a little pool after a year or two. This selection should remain compact, especially when their roots are contained in a pond basket (see p.117). Their preferred pond depth is the measurement from the top of the root ball to the water surface.

MARSH MARIGOLD *CALTHA PALUSTRIS*

HEIGHT AND SPREAD 24 × 18 in (60 × 45 cm)
POND DEPTH Water level to 3 in (8 cm)
HARDINESS Zones 3–7
SUN ☼ ☼

Also known as kingcup, this well-behaved pond plant bears bright yellow flowers on tall, branched stems for many weeks in late spring and early summer. The blooms are loved by bees and other pollinators, and appear among the bright green, kidney-shaped foliage. The stems often flop over after flowering, covering the water surface, so cut them back to keep the plant looking neat. This plant prefers shallow water and will also grow in boggy soil around the edges of a small pond.

Marsh marigold's yellow blooms appear among glossy kidney-shaped leaves in spring.

BOG ARUM *CALLA PALUSTRIS*

HEIGHT AND SPREAD 10 × 18 in (25 × 45 cm)
POND DEPTH 3–4 in (7.5–10 cm)
HARDINESS Zones 2–6
SUN ☼ ☼

The bog arum's network of heart-shaped leaves provides a foil for the elegant flower heads that push up between them in late spring. The blooms are made up of a greenish-white petal-like spathe and a spike of tiny green flowers, and are followed in summer by bright red berries. This perennial will die down in winter but pop up again in early spring. Keep it confined to a pond basket to limit its spread. All parts are poisonous, so this is not a good choice for those with water-loving pets.

Bog arum produces pretty greenish-white flower heads in spring, followed by red berries.

JAPANESE WATER IRIS *IRIS ENSATA*

HEIGHT AND SPREAD up to 36 × 24 in (90 × 60 cm)
POND DEPTH Water level
HARDINESS Zones 4–9
SUN ☼ ☼

Not to be confused with the Japanese iris (*I. laevigata*), a marginal plant that also grows in water but is much more vigorous, this less invasive species is ideal for the edges of a small pond. It comes in range of flower colors, including purple, pink, and white, while 'Variegata' has decorative green- and white-striped foliage. Happy with its roots in shallow water from spring to early fall, this iris may rot if it is wet over winter, so keep it in a basket and plant it in potting mix in the fall.

'Rose Queen' produces small lilac-pink flowers in summer that can be used as cut flowers.

MINIATURE WATER LILY *NYMPHAEA*

HEIGHT AND SPREAD 4 × 18 in (10 × 45 cm)
POND DEPTH 6–12 in (15–30 cm)
HARDINESS Zones 3–11
SUN ☀

Water lilies come in a range of sizes and some will cover a lake, so make sure you buy one of the miniature varieties for your tiny pond. Look for those with the name 'Pygmaea', which have been bred for small pools, or check the labels of others for sizes. These compact plants produce small flowers in a wide range of colors, including red, pink, yellow, and white, and some are lightly fragrant. Many have dark-patterned foliage, too. Water lilies must have sufficient sunlight to bloom.

The fragrant yellow flowers of 'Pygmaea Helvola' appear above purple and green leaves.

ARROWHEAD *SAGITTARIA SAGITTIFOLIA*

HEIGHT AND SPREAD 32 × 32 in (80 × 80 cm)
POND DEPTH 2–8 in (5–20 cm)
HARDINESS Zones 6–9
SUN ☀

Grown for its arrow-shaped bright green leaves, which appear quite late in spring from a tuber that pushes up above the soil, this plant is also known as the "swamp potato." In late summer, slim stems topped with small white flowers with dark pink centers, which are loved by bees, appear among the leaves. The only drawback with arrowhead is that it dies down after flowering so, if there is space, use other marginals such as a corkscrew rush to keep the interest going as fall approaches.

Distinctive arrow-shaped leaves give this beautiful leafy plant its common name.

CORKSCREW RUSH *JUNCUS EFFUSUS F. SPIRALIS*

HEIGHT AND SPREAD 20 × 20 in (50 × 50 cm)
POND DEPTH Water level
HARDINESS Zones 4–9
SUN ☀ ☀

Guaranteed to turn heads, this unusual little evergreen rush will decorate a small pond all year round with its slim, spiraling, leafless stems that look like curled green ribbons. Clusters of small, creamy-brown flowers also appear on the stems in summer. It is a generally trouble-free plant that will bulk up year on year, so confine it to a pond basket to keep it in check. You may find it also self-seeds in damp areas elsewhere in the garden, but unwanted seedlings are easily removed.

The spiraling stems of this unusual little rush create an eye-catching feature.

MINIATURE CATTAIL *TYPHA MINIMA*

HEIGHT AND SPREAD 24 × 18 in (60 × 45 cm)
POND DEPTH 1–4 in (2.5–10 cm)
HARDINESS Zones 3–10
SUN ☀

Like a full-size rush that's been shrunk in the laundry, this diminutive form produces slim grassy leaves and spikes of oval brown flowers, known as maces, in summer. Florists use these flowers in dried arrangements, so cut a few for the house. The miniature bulrush is a deciduous plant and will die back overwinter, but fresh new growth will return each spring. Plant it in a basket to limit its spread; it may self-seed in other damp spots, so keep an eye out for unwanted seedlings.

This rush bears small brown flower heads on slender stems for many months in summer.

FITTING IN FURNITURE

Comfortable seats and loungers allow you to relax and really enjoy your garden, while a dining set for family and friends to share al fresco meals is a must if you have the space. Choosing furniture that fits is, of course, a priority in a small space, but never compromise on comfort. Fit an L-shaped sofa between flowerbeds or on a patio, or install a bench along a boundary wall to save space in a tiny yard.

Compact, lightweight, metal-framed dining furniture provides the ideal solution for a balcony or roof terrace.

This purpose-built bench allows space beneath and behind it for a collection of shade-loving ferns.

SPACE INVADERS

When designing your small garden, plan your seating and dining areas carefully and choose your furniture before deciding upon the size of a patio or hard standing to ensure it will fit easily (see pp.32–33 for ideas on creating spaces for seating and dining). Do not forfeit comfort for size—tiny chairs or an inadequate number of seats for your household will limit your use and enjoyment of the space. For example, if your family comprises four people, a small patio with a tiny bistro set is unlikely to work for you and it may be worth reducing the size of planting beds or a lawn to accommodate a larger terrace and furniture that brings everyone together.

Plan some neat solutions to pack in plants around and under seating. Tuck shade-loving ferns under a bench or a hammock to provide a green frill at ground level, or set chairs on paving stones within a flowerbed to give you an up-close view of the flowers and the wildlife that visits them, helping you relax and unwind. If there is room, include a couple of seating areas that provide you with different views of your garden, patio, or terrace.

COMPACT SOLUTIONS

Think about how you can maximize the seating in your space. Solutions include long, purpose-built benches that extend along boundary walls, or wide coping on top of a solidly built raised bed that provides extra perching spots for party guests or for you to look at the flowers. Tables that can be extended when you are entertaining and stackable chairs will save precious space, while folding tables and director's chairs provide comfortable seating for visitors and can then be stored indoors when not in use. In tiny spaces, consider commissioning a craftsperson to make a wall-mounted, fold-down table or bench for occasional use.

Folding director's chairs are light and easy to move around, and can be stored indoors when not in use.

MATERIAL MATTERS

Lightweight aluminum- or stainless-steel-framed furniture is a good choice for a balcony or roof terrace where the load-bearing capacity must be considered. Furniture made from recycled light materials such as maritime plastic is another solution and helps reduce pollution levels—some pieces can be disassembled and recycled a second time after use. Heavier timber furniture is suitable for a small space, but check that the wood has Forest Stewardship Council (FSC) certification, confirming that it's from a responsibly managed forest. When buying sofas and chairs with cushions, check that the latter are waterproof; even if they are, you may find that the manufacturers recommend bringing them undercover in winter, so ensure you have a dry space to store them.

A folding stainless steel bistro set is easy to move around a small patio or roof terrace.

STORAGE SOLUTIONS

A small shed or storage unit to provide a home for essentials such as a mower and bicycles can double as a decorative feature if used as a prop for climbing plants or topped with a sedum roof. When calculating how much storage space you need, add a little extra to house other items you may accumulate over time. Make sure that any storage you install will be easy to access throughout the year.

Create a sedum roof on a small shed to transform it into a flowering wildlife feature to attract pollinating insects.

WHAT'S IN STORE?

Storage spaces will accommodate clutter such as children's toys and tools when not in use, and can also provide extra surfaces to dress up with ornaments or plants. You will need a watertight unit for a power mower, and for furniture cushions if you have no space to keep the latter over winter in your home.

Tiny slimline sheds are also useful on roof terraces, providing a home for potting mix, garden tools, and flowerpots that could make your home dirty if stored inside. Consider, too, the storage opportunities of areas under decks or beneath stairs to make the most of every available space.

Growing plants up the sides of a shed or creating a sedum roof on the top will help blend it into the outdoors. Sedum roofs can be bought from online specialists and are easy to install. After making an edging around the roof, you simply roll out the pre-planted matting over an underlay and cut it to fit.

Install slimline greenhouses next to a sunny warm fence or wall to protect tender crops such as tomatoes.

A WARM SPOT TO GROW

If you plan to grow a few vegetables, many tender types, including tomatoes, eggplants, and peppers, require protection from frost and can take up too much space indoors as they mature from seedlings started off on a windowsill. A lean-to greenhouse or free-standing structure set against a warm wall or fence will help solve this problem. Even an unheated unit may provide enough warmth at night to keep your plants safe from frost— covering them with a layer or two of recycled bubble plastic packaging will provide additional protection.

For a balcony or roof terrace, look for mini greenhouses and wall-mounted units, which will hold trays of tender seedlings and hothouse plants that need extra protection even in summer in cooler climates.

This clever narrow storage unit runs along the length of a small patio and looks like a fence when closed.

SITING YOUR FEATURE

Whether you are buying a shed, storage box, or tiny greenhouse, think carefully about where you are going to install it. If you want to store a bicycle, for example, make sure the shed has easy access to a gate or side passage leading on to the road. A shed for tools and a mower can be tucked away at the back in shade, or position it in a sunnier spot where it can also act as screening, providing shelter for plants or privacy for an informal seating area. Greenhouses will require a sunny site to ensure your tender crops receive the rays they need to ripen the fruits. Lay a paved or gravel path that provides access to your shed or greenhouse and, ideally, is wide enough for a wheelbarrow.

Paint your shed a color that complements your design and use it to create a sheltered seating area, too.

LIGHTING THE WAY

Lighting your space not only extends the time you can spend outside, it can also elevate the design with theatrical effects. Illuminated trees, ornaments, and fountains become sparkling features as dusk falls, while steps and paths are made safer with lights to show the way. Just remember to turn unnecessary lights off when you go inside to minimize pollution, which can adversely affect wildlife.

Soft, glowing LEDs can transform a daytime garden into a magical evening space of light and shadow.

LED lights set into the risers of a flight of steps make them safe at night, while also creating a decorative effect.

THEATRICAL EFFECTS

Using theatrical lighting effects in a small yard or on a roof terrace will help to increase the drama. Spotlights covered by cowls or "eyelids" create a soft glow over planting at ground level, or angle them upward to illuminate a tree trunk or graze the surface of a textured wall. Strings of small bulbs threaded through a tree canopy will create a starlit effect, or use them to highlight the leaf shapes and colors of a large shrub. If you have a fountain, illuminating it will throw spangles of light around as the beams catch the water droplets.

Strings of colored lights can produce a party ambience, and color-changing LEDs will produce interesting effects in a water feature, but most garden designers recommend "warm white" bulbs to enhance plants and ornaments.

Angle a spotlight up a tree to illuminate the trunk and leafy stems.

PRACTICAL MATTERS

The most important parts of the space to illuminate are the seating and dining areas, making them usable in the evenings, and steps and pathways, where lighting will help prevent trips and falls. Install lights on each side of your steps or within the risers, so that only the treads are illuminated and the lights won't dazzle you as you walk up or down them. Remember to illuminate the top step, too. The same technique works well for paths where beams are angled onto the ground rather than lighting the whole area, conveying a sense of mystery while minimizing light pollution.

In very small spaces, you may need only one light or a string of bulbs above a seating area, and on a balcony, you can make use of indoor lights to augment those outside. Whichever lighting you choose, do not overdo it. One of the charms of a nighttime garden is the magical quality a few strategically placed spotlights create; flooding the whole area with security-type lighting will look harsh and feel uncomfortable, especially if the beams are directed at eye level.

LIGHTING OPTIONS

Your choice of lighting in a small space ranges from traditional candles to LEDs and solar-powered features. Live flames offer a romantic ambience and look pretty on a dining table, but keep them away from plants and flammable items, and protect them from the breeze with glass holders or lanterns.

Good-quality LEDs are the best option for yards and terraces, since they are long-lasting, cheap to run, and offer the most reliable and flexible light source. You can plug them into an outdoor electricity supply, installed by a qualified electrician, or buy portable lamps with rechargeable batteries, which you charge indoors just like a phone or laptop and then bring outside.

Professionally designed and installed whole-yard lighting systems can be controlled by an app on your phone or panel inside your home, and you can also ask your supplier to include more than one circuit, allowing you to select specific areas to light up, and dimmers that control the glow. These systems are not cheap to install, but should ensure a beautifully lit yard, and the fittings and features can last for many years.

Solar-powered lights may seem like the most eco-friendly solution, but they have their limitations. The solar unit must be positioned in full sun for the lights to recharge, and most produce only a soft, decorative glow which may not be powerful enough to illuminate paths or dining areas. Cheap strings of novelty solar lights also tend to break easily and

Strings of LED lights are simply plugged into an outdoor electrical socket in a yard or on a roof terrace or balcony.

often stop working after a season or two, and because they comprise many different materials, they can't be recycled and frequently end up in a landfill.

Candles protected by glass lanterns provide a flexible lighting option and create a romantic ambience.

Water plants in pots from spring to fall, even after rain, since the leaves often shield the soil, leaving it dry.

MAINTAINING SMALL GARDEN SPACES

All gardens require some maintenance, and tiny spaces filled with plants in pots may need more attention than larger plots where plants are in the ground. To keep yours healthy, use the simple watering methods and systems described in this chapter, and ward off attacks from pests and diseases by checking plants regularly and treating any problems that arise without delay. Learning how to prune is also worthwhile, since some plants, including clematis and roses, put on their best shows after an annual cut.

HOW TO WATER AND FEED YOUR PLANTS

All plants need water to survive but many, once established, will get all they need from the rain that falls. However, young plants, those in pots, and annual crops will require additional irrigation. Likewise, mature plants tend not to need feeding if they're growing in the ground, especially if you apply an annual organic mulch (see p.17), but young and potted plants will need extra food to keep them healthy.

When watering young plants, use a can fitted with a rose head or set a hose on a gentle spray and target the soil, rather than the flowers, stems, and leaves.

WATERING WISDOM

Plants with established root systems that are growing in the ground can usually tap into the moist layers at lower depths, allowing them to survive dry spells, but young plants and annual crops with smaller roots are unable to fend for themselves in the same way, and will require watering. Use a can or hose, or, if you have many young plants or crops in a bed, water them with a leaky or drip hose. Attach these hoses to an outdoor faucet and lay them on the soil around your plants; they will slowly administer water to the soil above the plants' roots, resulting in very little waste.

Any plant in a pot, except a cactus or succulent, will require regular watering, too. Again, you can water by hand, or install an automatic watering system, which consists of a controller unit that you affix to the tap and hoses fitted with drippers that you insert into the potting mix. Then simply program the controller to regulate watering times. You can also attach a leaky hose to a controller to water the garden.

Always use tap water on seedlings because it is sterile and will protect them against disease. For other plants, use either tap water or, if watering by hand, rainwater from a barrel (see *opposite*) to minimize water wastage.

An automatic watering system ensures your pots are watered regularly even when you are away from home.

The best times to water are when evaporation rates are low, either in the early morning or later in the evening.

WATERING CONTAINERS

The key to irrigating containerized plants is to give them a long drink every few days rather than applying little and often. A good dose of water will ensure the roots grow down into the pot to reach the moisture, while a sprinkling on top will encourage them to grow up to the surface where they will be more

Leave a space between the top of the potting mix and the pot rim to prevent water from spilling over the sides.

vulnerable to drying out. Leave a gap of 1–2 in (3–5 cm) between the potting mix and the rim of the pot to allow water to pool there and then percolate down into the soil. Fit a rose head onto a watering can or use a gentle spray setting on a hose and each time you water, apply enough to pool on top of the potting mix; leave this to drain and then add more when watering a large pot. Make sure your containers have good drainage to prevent waterlogging, and add a layer of gravel or aggregates over the surface to help trap the moisture below.

SAVING RESOURCES

In a small yard or on a roof terrace, install an outdoor faucet to make watering easier and more convenient, and also include a rain barrel affixed to the house roof downspout and to any sheds or outbuildings. Most plants prefer rainwater and it conserves this precious resource. Choose a slimline unit suitable for a tiny space, and ensure that the overflow goes into a flowerbed, especially on a roof where flooding could damage the properties below. Also check that a full barrel will not exceed the roof's load-bearing capacity.

> **TOP TIP** LAWNS WILL SURVIVE LONG PERIODS OF DROUGHT WITHOUT EXTRA IRRIGATION, SO PUT AWAY THE SPRINKLER TO SAVE PRECIOUS WATER RESOURCES. EVEN IF THE GRASS TURNS YELLOW, IT WILL GREEN UP AGAIN A FEW DAYS AFTER IT RAINS.

Apply an organic seaweed fertilizer to crops and plants growing in containers a few weeks after planting.

FOOD FOR THOUGHT

Research by the Royal Horticultural Society in the UK has shown that nutrient deficiencies in garden soils are very rare and that most mature plants will thrive without extra fertilizers. So, if you are applying an annual mulch of organic matter and you have matched your plants with the conditions in your space, you probably will not need to feed your established plants. However, plants in pots and young crops will require extra food from time to time.

Most commercial potting mixes contain some nutrients so, for the most part, you will not need to add any more for about 6–8 weeks after planting. If growing annual crops, you can then add a slow-release granular fertilizer to nourish your plants for the rest of the season, or apply an organic seaweed feed every two or three weeks in summer and early fall. Use a fertilizer with a high potassium content, such as a tomato feed, for flowering plants or fruiting crops such as tomatoes and peppers.

For shrubs, trees, and other long-term plants in containers, feed annually in spring. Carefully remove the top layer of potting mix from the pot, taking care not to damage the roots, and replace with fresh potting mix plus all-purpose granular fertilizer (check the label for application rates).

Install a small rain barrel to the downspout of a shed to capture rainwater that you can use to irrigate your plants.

WISE WEEDING

The adage that says a weed is simply a plant in the wrong place has some truth, but invasive species such as bindweed and ground elder are rarely in the right place and are best dealt with promptly to save your other plants from being swamped. While some weeds, including nettles, daisies, and buttercups, offer forage for beneficial insects, allowing too many to invade your garden could harm other wildlife by reducing biodiversity if they take over. Try compromising by removing vigorous types and allowing a few easy-to-extract weeds to coexist with crops and ornamentals.

Pulling out the top growth every week can help control bindweed where the roots are too extensive to dig out.

WHY WEED?

Weeds are highly efficient plants that grow quickly, covering the soil with a blanket of foliage and flowers and extending their reach by setting vast numbers of seeds or invading new ground via their root networks. They steal water, light, and space from your ornamental plants and crops, robbing them of their basic needs, which may either kill them or impede their growth. Some weeds are also hosts for plant pests and diseases (see p.138).

The best way to deal with weeds is to familiarize yourself with the mature plants and seedlings and remove them swiftly before they can spread or do any major damage.

The leaves of lawn weeds such as daisies (*Bellis perennis*) and germander speedwell (*Veronica chamaedrys*) can kill surrounding grass by shading it, but these plants are both good food sources for pollinating insects, including bees, so you may wish to tolerate a few rather than digging them all out or resorting to chemical treatments.

Removing the long tap root from dandelions prevents regrowth and is easier when plants are young.

WEEDING METHODS

Prevention is better than cure when it comes to tackling weeds. Laying a mulch over the soil helps prevent them taking root, and while some weeds may germinate in the mulching layer, they will be easier to remove. Growing ornamental plants and crops close together, so they form a leafy canopy over the soil, also prevents weed seeds from landing on the surface and will steal the light and weaken any that do germinate.

Inevitably, some weeds will make it through your defenses and need to be removed. Hoe off annuals and pull up or dig out perennials; avoid herbicides, which damage the environment and rarely do much to solve the problem, since weeds always return.

Hoe on a sunny, dry day, pushing the blade back and forth just beneath the soil surface to sever the top growth from the roots. Leave the weeds on the soil to wither. Some perennial weeds can be pulled up, but many will need to be dug out to remove all of the roots, since any tiny pieces left in the soil may regrow into a new plant. Cover heavily infested areas with an old carpet or opaque plastic sheet for six months to a year to remove the light and kill off the weeds. Where weeds are growing too close to your plants to dig out, remove the top growth and then keep pulling up any new shoots that appear. This will weaken and eventually kill the weed, if you are vigilant.

Hoe off annual and young perennial weeds by pushing the sharp blade just beneath the soil surface.

IDENTIFYING COMMON WEEDS

Recognizing weeds that grow in your garden will help you identify and remove them promptly before they spread. Also take note of the seedlings, the leaves of which may look slightly different to those of the mature plants.

Green alkanet (Pentaglottis sempervirens)

Hairy-leaved, blue-flowered, evergreen perennial; spreads by seed.

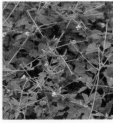

Wood avens (Geum urbanum)

Perennial with rounded leaves and buttercup-like flowers; spreads by roots and seed.

Couch grass (Elymus repens)

Coarse, grasslike green leaves; spreads via wiry white roots, which form dense clumps.

Bindweed (Calystegia sepium)

Twining perennial climber with white trumpet flowers; spreads via seed, rhizomes, and long aerial shoots.

Ground elder (Aegopodium podagraria)

Perennial with divided green leaves and lacy white summer flowers; spreads via roots.

Lesser celandine (Ficaria verna)

Perennial bulb with glossy round leaves and yellow spring flowers; spreads via bulbs and seed.

Dock (Rumex obtusifolius)

Perennial with broad green leaves and spikes of small red summer flowers; spreads via seed.

Horsetail (Equisetum arvense)

Evergreen fern with striped stems and bottlebrush-like foliage; spreads via roots and spores.

Nettles (Urtica dioica)

Perennial with hairy, stinging green leaves and dangling cream flower heads; spreads via roots and seed.

PRUNING YOUR PLANTS

Pruning woody plants such as trees and shrubs helps keep them healthy by removing dead or diseased stems, while also improving their shape and, in some cases, encouraging more flowering and fruiting stems to form. Perennials that have stood over winter should be cut back in spring to make way for new growth to push through, while deadheading flowering plants in spring and summer can prolong their display by promoting the development of new buds.

Reduce the weight of heavy tree branches by removing them in stages before cutting about 2 in (5 cm) from the trunk.

Cutting back the stems of buddleia hard in spring will encourage the plant to form more flowering shoots.

WHEN TO PRUNE

Most shrubs and climbers that flower before early or midsummer should be pruned just after they have finished flowering, but those that flower later in the year will need to be cut back in early spring. This is because early-flowering shrubs generally develop their flower buds on stems produced the year before they bloom, while later-flowering plants develop buds on stems that they have produced in the same year. Cutting back the stems of buddleias, hardy fuchsias, and late summer-flowering clematis to about 12 in (30 cm) from the ground in spring will encourage more flowering stems to develop, and also restrict the height of these plants. There are exceptions to the rules, however, so check each individual plant to discover when to prune them. For example, large-flowered clematis hybrids that bloom in early summer should be cut back lightly to the first or second healthy bud in early spring, not after flowering.

Most trees are pruned when dormant in winter. The exceptions are trees in the *Prunus* genus, including cherries and plums, which should be pruned in summer to prevent silver leaf disease. Others, including birch (*Betula*), hornbeams (*Carpinus*), and magnolias, should be pruned in the fall or early winter because they bleed sap if cut from late winter to mid-spring.

TOP TIP BEFORE PRUNING A TREE, MAKE SURE IT IS ON YOUR PROPERTY, AND THAT FALLING LIMBS WILL NOT POSE A HAZARD.

WHAT TO PRUNE

When pruning, first remove dead and diseased stems, cutting them down to the base of the plant or back to healthy wood. Then remove stems that are crossing or rubbing others, which can create wounds that open the plant up to infections. Finally, prune stems that have outgrown their space, and remove growth to create a more open canopy so that light reaches the center of the plant. Removing the tip of a stem also stimulates the growth of side stems lower down, which can help create a bushier plant. Use this technique on young shrubs to encourage branching or on spindly older plants.

Cut out crossing stems that may rub against others and create open wounds vulnerable to infection.

In early spring, cut back grasses such as miscanthus and perennial plants to the ground.

CUTTING BACK PERENNIALS

The dead stems and seed heads of grasses and perennial plants that remain intact over winter help decorate the garden at this time of year, but they will need to be cut back in early spring to make way for new growth. Simply prune the old, dried stems down to the ground, using sharp shears for large swathes or pruners for smaller groups of plants. Running your fingers through grasses also helps remove old leaves. Also try chopping the clippings into smaller sections and leave them on the surface to create a weed-suppressing mulch.

Pinch out the faded flowers of annuals such as *Impatiens* every few days to encourage more blooms to develop.

MAKING MORE FLOWERS

Cutting off the dead or dying flowers of annuals, perennials, and some shrubs can encourage the plant to produce more blooms, extending the display. You can remove the flower heads of perennials by simply snapping them off with your fingers or cutting the stems with scissors or pruners. Use sharp pruners to remove the flower heads of woody-stemmed plants such as roses, cutting the stems down to healthy buds below them. Deadheading regularly keeps plants looking neat, too, but it will prevent berries or hips from forming, so keep some flowers intact if you want these to develop.

HOW TO PRUNE

Always wear gloves when pruning and use clean, sharp cutting tools, such as pruners for stems the width of a pencil or smaller, or a pruning saw, telescopic ratchet loppers, or anvil loppers for larger stems. Call in a professional tree surgeon or arboriculturist to cut large branches from trees or shrubs above head height or to carry out major restorative work.

To make a pruning cut, locate the buds (raised bumps or small shoots) on your plant's stem. If they are set alternately along the stem, make a slanting cut just above one of them, so that rain will drain away from it. If the buds are in opposite pairs, make a straight cut just above them.

Make a slanting cut above a bud so rain will drain away from it.

Make a straight cut above a pair of opposite buds.

PEST PREVENTION

Pests can ruin plants and crops, but there are some easy ways to keep them under control and prevent infestations. Making sure that plants are healthy will, in some cases, help them stave off attacks, while luring pest predators to your garden offers an eco-friendly way of reducing their impact. Another effective control is to make regular inspections of vulnerable plants such as lilies and remove pests before they inflict any damage. Growing plants in hanging baskets or on windowsills where flightless pests can't get to them easily will also help protect the most vulnerable.

Check lilies for bright red lily beetles and pick off any you see; they feed in groups, so look for others if you spot one.

ON THE DEFENSE

Mature, healthy plants can often ward off pest attacks or continue to thrive with just a few munched leaves, while other plants, including geums, Japanese anemones, many ferns, and herbs, are rarely troubled by pests of any kind. Filling your garden with these tough, pest-resistant species will make your life easier, but if you want to introduce vulnerable seedlings, plants with succulent flower buds, and crops that provide forage for specific insects, such as cabbage white butterfly larvae, you will need a strategy to keep pests at bay.

The best eco-friendly method is to introduce an army of insect-eating allies to wage war on your plant pests. Birds, frogs, toads, hoverflies, lacewing larvae, and both the adults and larvae of ladybugs provide a formidable force for good in the garden. Blackbirds, thrushes, frogs, and toads enjoy a diet of slugs and snails, while sparrow chicks and insect predators like to feast on aphids, which threaten the health of many garden plants. Include a small pool to lure amphibians to your garden and add some pollen-rich plants to entice adult hoverflies and lacewings. Ladybugs will find their own way into your garden when they discover that aphids are on the menu, appearing as soon as the numbers of these sap-sucking pests start to swell.

Familiarize yourself with ladybug larvae, which are your allies in the fight against aphid attacks.

Frogs love to feast on slugs and snails and will help keep the numbers of these voracious plant pests in check.

Close cousins of aphids, whiteflies feast on rose buds and should be removed promptly before they distort the flowers.

REGULAR INSPECTIONS

Inspecting plants for signs of pests often pays dividends. Look under lily leaves every day or two for signs of the slow-moving red lily beetles, which are easy to spot and catch. Wipe off any of their orangey-red eggs, too. Check flower buds, leaves, and stems for aphids and remove any you find with a blast of water from a hose or by squashing them with your fingers (use a glove or tissue if you're squeamish). Also watch out for vine weevils, which are gray beetle-like insects that move slowly and make U-shaped holes in leaf edges. If plants suddenly collapse, check the soil or potting mix for the weevils' C-shaped cream-colored larvae, which do most of the damage by eating plants' roots, and if they are present, try a biological control (see p.136). Slugs and snails are often too numerous for pest predators to control completely, so hunt for them during the day. You will find them hiding beneath leaves or stones, or behind furniture; collect them and place them near a pond to feed the frogs and toads, if you don't want to squash them. Throwing them over the fence rarely works; they simply return.

ORGANIC PESTICIDES

You may be tempted by organic pesticides that claim to prevent or cure pest infestations. Neem oil is said to deter as well as kill pests, while other products made from natural materials such as pyrethrum (derived from chrysanthemum and *Tanacetum coccineum* plants) or soaps can help control aphids, thrips, and other pests. However, while these products won't cause pollution, they are nonspecific, which means that they may also harm beneficial insects, including hoverflies and ladybug larvae.

TOP TIP SEEDLINGS AND YOUNG PLANTS ARE PARTICULARLY VULNERABLE TO ATTACKS FROM SLUGS AND SNAILS, SO KEEP THEM INDOORS OR OUT OF HARM'S WAY UNTIL THEY HAVE DEVELOPED PEST-RESISTANT STURDY STEMS.

Some organic pesticides are made from pyrethrum, which is extracted from *Tanacetum coccineum* plants.

PEST CONTROL

When pest predators (*see p.134*) cannot cope with the sheer numbers of pests in your small space, you may have to resort to other methods of control to safeguard your plants. Try to avoid chemical pesticides, which can affect other wildlife and will damage the environment, and use methods that target the specific pests that are threatening your plants rather than the wider insect population. Also consider how much pest damage you can tolerate—a few munched leaves are difficult to spot in a bed full of flowers and may require no control, thereby reducing your workload.

Nematodes are mixed with water and applied to vulnerable plants when pests are active from spring to early fall.

BIOLOGICAL CONTROL

This organic method of control employs tiny insect predators to eat plant pests. Biological controls do not harm the environment or other wildlife and are a good choice for organic gardeners. The most popular are microscopic nematodes, which control slugs, vine weevils, and other pests, and parasitic wasps that eat aphids. Buy biological controls online or order them from a garden center and store in the refrigerator until you are ready to use them. Mix them with water and apply from spring to early fall when pests are most active. Traps containing nematodes that control adult vine weevils should be placed on the ground in summer below plants showing the signs of weevil damage (see *opposite*).

PLANT BARRICADES

An easy way to prevent pests from eating your plants is to cover them with insect- or bird-proof netting. This will protect soft fruits from garden birds keen to eat your crops, and cabbages and other brassicas from pigeon damage and cabbage white butterflies, the larvae of which can completely destroy these vegetables. Drape the netting over canes or wire hoops to hold it away from the leaves and flowers, and peg it down on the soil to seal off all routes in.

Wool-based barrier products can help to deter slugs and snails from attacking young plants. Some gardeners also find that sharp, gritty materials deter these pests, which dislike the textures and are not keen to cross them, although you may find that some may still venture over if the rewards are worth the effort.

Cover carrots and parsley with insect-proof netting to protect them from the carrot fly, which eats the roots.

Bury a jam jar and fill it with beer to attract slugs and snails, which then fall in and drown.

PEST TRAPS

Gardeners have been trapping slugs and snails in jars of beer for centuries, and this age-old, tried and trusted method still has value in a modern garden. Bury a jam jar or similar container in the soil close to vulnerable plants, with the rim level with the soil surface, then fill it with beer. The pests will be attracted to the brew and will drown when they fall in.

If earwigs are eating your dahlias, try setting inverted pots stuffed with straw on canes close to your plants. The earwigs will crawl in during the day and you can then dispose of them.

Use sticky or pheromone traps during spring to snare pests such as sap-sucking whitefly in greenhouses or codling moth on apple trees.

COMMON PESTS

ANTS
Although ants rarely do much harm to plants, their nests can be a nuisance in pots. Ants feed on the sweet residue that aphids deposit and can encourage infestations of these more harmful sap-sucking insects by guarding them against predators such as ladybugs. Removing the aphids and their residue will help reduce the numbers of ants running up and down on your plants.

APHIDS
These tiny sap-sucking pests are usually green or black, but some are yellow, pink, white, or mottled. They cause distorted buds and stems, sometimes killing the host plant when an infestation occurs. Remove them with a jet of water, use a tissue to wipe them off, or try a biological control.

EARWIGS
Nocturnal insects with pincers on their hindquarters, earwigs eat the flowers and leaves of clematis, dahlias, and chrysanthemums. Pick them off in the evening, or trap them in upturned flowerpots filled with dry grass set on sticks close to your vulnerable plants.

LILY BEETLES
Both the bright red adult beetles and their black excrement-coated grubs can devastate lilies and fritillarias by eating the foliage. Check lilies every day or two, pick off the beetles, and wipe off their orange-red eggs and larvae.

SLUGS AND SNAILS
No garden will be completely free of these nocturnal creatures, also known as mollusks, which can reduce flourishing plants to bare stems in just one night. They prefer young plants, so protect these indoors or set them on a table outside until the stems have toughened up. Safeguard other vulnerable plants such as hostas by setting traps, laying gritty materials (see *opposite*) around the stems, or using a biological control or slug pellets based on iron phosphate.

VINE WEEVILS
Adult vine weevils are slow-moving beetles that make U-shaped holes in the leaves of a variety of plants but do little damage. However, their C-shaped cream larvae, which are about ½ in (15 mm) in length, eat roots and can quickly kill a plant. Pick off the adults or use biological controls to keep both adults and grubs in check.

Ants will protect colonies of aphids.

Aphids can kill plants by eating the sap.

Earwigs munch on flowers.

Lily beetles eat lily and fritillary leaves.

Slugs and snails eat many plants.

Vine weevil grubs eat plant roots.

DEALING WITH DISEASES

Plants growing in the conditions they enjoy will generally have greater immunity to diseases than those struggling to survive, so minimize the risks by keeping yours as healthy as possible. However, diseases such as blackspot in roses can infect thriving plants as well as sickly ones, and they will need to be managed, even if they can't be eliminated. In many countries, legislation has limited the use of chemical treatments that have been shown to adversely affect wildlife and the environment, which means that gardeners must look for new ways to prevent and control plant diseases.

The wilted leaves of this young rhododendron are due to drought and it will soon revive after watering.

DISEASE-BUSTERS

The first step to managing a plant disease is to identify what is afflicting your plant. In some cases, symptoms such as wilting or yellow- or red-tinted leaves are the result of insufficient water or nutrients and the plant will quickly recover after a drink or feed, so try these measures first before diagnosing a more serious problem.

Plant diseases are often carried by fungal spores in the air or in water droplets that splash up on to a plant from the soil. Fungal diseases also affect the roots and stems of plants grown in damp soil conditions. Ensuring good air flow around plants, avoiding overhead watering, and making sure your soil or potting mix has good drainage will help minimize the risks. Mulching can also reduce the spread of some diseases by improving the growing conditions and covering fungal spores so they can't splash up onto a plant.

Where a particular plant-specific disease is widespread, such as rose black spot or blight in tomatoes, choose cultivars bred with some disease resistance. Check plants for signs of disease before buying and reject any that have discolored leaves or flowers.

Tomato blight is an incurable fungal disease that causes the fruits to turn brown and then rot.

Weeds such as groundsel often carry rust spores that may affect crops or vulnerable plants such as hollyhocks.

HOW DISEASES SPREAD

Many diseases are spread by plant pests, such as aphids and other sap-sucking insects, so remove them as soon as you see them (see p.137). Some weeds, including groundsel and goosefoot, also carry diseases and viruses and should be removed promptly to prevent any infections from spreading. Diseases such as box blight can be spread via cutting tools, so wipe the blades after use on each plant with hot water and soap or detergent. Also pick up diseased leaves from the ground to prevent spores settling on the soil, and clean muddy boots that may be harboring infections.

COMMON PLANT DISEASES

These are some of the most common plant diseases; acquainting yourself with the symptoms and causes may help you prevent future outbreaks.

BLACK SPOT *Symptoms*: Purple or black spots that may have a yellow aura around them appear on the upper leaf surfaces. The leaves then fall off and this can weaken plants. Black marks may also appear on stems.
Control: Collect and destroy fallen leaves in the fall, or bury under a layer of mulch. Remove affected stems in spring before the leaves appear. Buy disease-resistant cultivars. Fungicides are also available.

DOWNY MILDEW *Symptoms*: Discolored leaves on the upper surfaces and white, gray, or purple mold below.
Control: Remove infected parts. The spores are transmitted in wet weather and when humidity is high. Water in the morning so leaves can dry during the day, avoid overhead watering, and improve ventilation around plants.

GRAY MOLD (BOTRYTIS) *Symptoms*: This fungal disease (*Botrytis cinerea*) causes fuzzy gray-brown mold on decaying leaves, stems, flowers, and fruits. Living plants' buds and flowers are also affected and may shrivel and die.
Control: It is often caused by high humidity, so provide better ventilation and drainage. Remove dead plant material promptly when it drops on to the soil or compost.

POTATO AND TOMATO BLIGHT *Symptoms*: A white fungal growth develops on the undersides of the leaves, which then shrivel and turn brown. Brown patches appear on ripening tomatoes, while potato tubers turn reddish-brown beneath the skins and rot.
Control: Burn infected material—do not compost it. Practice crop rotation and buy disease-resistant varieties. Indoor tomatoes are rarely affected.

POWDERY MILDEW *Symptoms*: A white powdery fungal growth covers the leaves, flowers, and fruits, which may then become distorted.

Control: Remove infected parts and improve air flow by spacing plants more widely. Add mulches over the soil to retain water and improve drainage.

RUST *Symptoms*: Raised rusty brown, orange, and yellow pustules on lower leaf surfaces. Heavy infection reduces the vigor of plants; in others, it has little effect on fruiting and flowering and will not need any control.
Control: Where infection is localized, remove infected material, but do not take off too many leaves, which will affect growth. Clear away dead and diseased leaves on the soil in the fall; do not compost them.

VIRUSES *Symptoms*: Yellow or pale green spots, streaks, or mosaic patterns appear on the leaves. Flowers are smaller than usual and may be distorted or streaked with white patches; fruit may also be discolored and streaked.
Control: Remove and destroy infected material—do not compost. Remove weeds and control pests, such as aphids, which carry viruses. Wash hands after handling infected plants.

Black spot on rose leaves is unsightly but may not affect flowering.

Rust infects many plants, including hollyhocks and irises.

Powdery mildew is exacerbated by poor ventilation.

INDEX

Bold text indicates a main entry for the subject.

Author Zia Allaway

AUTHOR ACKNOWLEDGMENTS

Many thanks to Marek Walisiewicz at Cobalt id for commissioning me to write this book and to Paul Reid for his beautiful designs. Thanks also to editor Diana Vowles, and to the team at Dorling Kindersley for their help in fine-tuning the words.

PUBLISHER ACKNOWLEDGMENTS

DK would like to thank Mary-Clare Jerram for developing the original concept, Chris Young for content origination, Nicola Powling for jacket development, Margaret McCormack for indexing, and Paul Reid, Marek Walisiewicz, and the Cobalt team for their hard work in putting this book together.

PICTURE CREDITS

The publisher would like to thank the following for their kind permission to reproduce their photographs:

Alamy Stock Photo: A Garden 30tr, 33bl, 120cl; Aleksandr Volkov 75tl; Alison Thompson 111br; Andreas von Einsiedel 2c, 21bl, 25t, 31bl, 33bc, 44br; Anja Schaefer 13c; anne green-armytage flower pictures 19c; Bailey-Cooper Photography 32cr, 85tl; Bax Walker 123b; BIOSPHOTO 9bl, 50br; blickwinkel 26br, 62br, 91br, 119tr, 132cl; Botanic World 51tl; Botany vision 64br; Chris Clark 14bl, 25bl; Clare Gainey 96bl, 130tr; CRAIG BALLINGER 38bl; David Norton 134bl; David Winger 41bl; Deborah Vernon 52bl; Derek Harris 21tr; Elizabeth Whiting & Associates 89tr, 116tr; Ellen Rooney 38cr; Eye Ubiquitous 28tl; Fir Mamat 131tr; flowerphotos 93tl; FlowerStock 134tr; Gay Bumgarner 9tl; Geo-grafika 8cl; Guy Bell 40cl; Helen Sessions 11br; Holmes Garden Photos 18c, 49tl; Image Source 126c; Jane Geoghegan 125bc; Jane Tregelles 86bl; Jason Smalley Photography 55cr; Joe 12tr; John Glover 12cr; John Richmond 20t, 66tl; Kathy deWitt 34tr, 69tl; Mabo 120tr; Magdalena Bujak 38tr; Magdalena Iordache 63tl; Marc Boettcher 53tr, 112tr; Marcin Rogozinski 15c; Martyn Annetts 122cr; Matthew Bruce 32bl; McPhoto/Rolf Mueller 80tl; Melany Wood-Pearce 120br; Mick House 89bl; mike jarman 124tr, 124cl, 124br; Mike Twigg, fotocapricorn 129bl; Miriam Heppell 24tr; MISCELLANEOUSTOCK 111tl; Natalia Rüdisüli 9br; P Tomlins 50tr; P.Spiro 24bl; Panther Media GmbH 56cr; Pavlo Balanenko 26tl; Peter D Anderson 4c; Photiconix 136bc; Richard Garvey-Williams 134br; RM Floral 79bl; Robert Kneschke 12bc; Roberto Nistri 93tr; Roger Cracknell 01/classic 8cr; ronstik 125tr; Sergey Trifonov 98tr; Steffen Hauser / botanikfoto 65tl; Stuart Blyth 54bl; Suzanne Goodwin 30cl; Tim Gainey 112cl; TINA BROUGH 46b; Tom Ridout 8tr; Tony Giammarino 21br, 122bl; Victoria Ashman 121bc; Vladimir Fedorov 67bl; Westend61 GmbH 82c; Wlodzimierz Dondzik 133tl; Yon Marsh Natural History 139bc.

Dorling Kindersley: Alan Buckingham 114br, 115cl, 133cr, 139br; Brian North 83cl, 83cr, 83bl; Brian North / RHS Chelsea Flower Show 2009 22c, 57c; Brian North / RHS Chelsea Flower Show 2011 106tr; Brian North / RHS Hampton Court Flower Show 2009 28br, 31tl; Brian North / RHS Hampton Court Flower Show 2011 42br; Brian North / RHS Hampton Court Flower Show 2012 30cr, 34br, 55br; Brian North / Thompson and Morgan 97bl; Peter Anderson / RHS Hampton Court Flower Show 11tl; Dreamstime.com: Edward Phillips 137cl; iStock: Peopleimages 55cl; Mark Winwood / Ball Colegrave 73tr, 78br, 84tr, 86tl, 96tr, 96br, 97tl, 98tl, 98br, 99tr; Mark Winwood / Crug Farm 70tr; Mark Winwood / Downderry Nursery 92bl; Mark Winwood / Hadlow College 66bl; Mark Winwood / Hampton Court Flower Show 2014 99tl, 99br; Mark Winwood / Lullingstone Castle, Kent 86tr; Mark Winwood / Marle Place Gardens and Gallery, Brenchley, Kent 49bl; Mark Winwood / RHS Chelsea Flower Show 2014 62tr, 81bl; Mark Winwood / RHS Hampton Court Flower Show 2005, Designed by Guildford College, 'Journey of the Senses' 74cl; Mark Winwood / RHS Wisley 16br, 31br, 39br, 50tl, 51bl, 53br, 58bl, 58br, 60tl, 61tl, 61bl, 61tr, 64tl, 64tr, 64bl, 66br, 67tr, 67br, 78bl, 79tr, 81tl, 85tr, 85bl, 85br, 87tl, 87bl, 92tl, 92tr, 92br, 93br, 97tr, 105tr; Mark Winwood / Temple Newsam Estate, Leeds City Council 39bc; Peter Anderson 27c, 28tr, 33br, 48bl, 49br, 52br; Peter Anderson / RHS Chelsea Flower Show 2009 29c, 43br; Peter Anderson / RHS Chelsea Flower Show 2011 10cl, 18bl; Peter Anderson / RHS Hampton Court Flower Show 102cr, 106bl; Peter Anderson / RHS Hampton Court Flower Show 2009 102tr; Peter Anderson / RHS Hampton Court Flower Show 2010 109tr, 111tr, 112br; Peter Anderson / RHS Hampton Court Flower Show 2014 17tr; RHS Tatton Park 61br, 87br.

GAP Photos: Elke Borkowski 6c; Friedrich Strauss 83tl; Howard Rice - 32, St Barnabas Road, Cambridge 116bc; Jerry Harpur - Design: Donald Walsh 89tl; Martin Hughes-Jones 113tr; Suzie Gibbons 88br.

Getty Images: Jacky Parker Photography 44tr, 86br; Johner Images 45br.

Illustrations by Cobalt id.

All other images © Dorling Kindersley

Produced for DK by
COBALT ID

Managing Editor Marek Walisiewicz
Editor Diana Vowles
Managing Art Editor Paul Reid
Art Editor Darren Bland

DK LONDON
Project Editor Amy Slack
Senior US Editor Megan Douglass
Editor Lucy Sienkowska
Senior Designer Glenda Fisher
Managing Editor Ruth O'Rourke
Managing Art Editor Marianne Markham
Production Editor David Almond
Production Controller Stephanie McConnell
Jacket Designer Amy Cox
Jacket Co-ordinator Jasmin Lennie
Art Director Maxine Pedliham
Publisher Katie Cowan

First American Edition, 2023
Published in the United States by DK Publishing
1745 Broadway, 20th Floor, New York, NY 10019

Copyright © 2023 Dorling Kindersley Limited
DK, a Division of Penguin Random House LLC
23 24 25 26 27 10 9 8 7 6 5 4 3 2 1
001–333476–Jan/2023

A catalog record for this book
is available from the Library of Congress.
ISBN 978-0-7440-6957-0

DK books are available at special discounts when purchased in bulk for sales promotions, premiums, fund-raising, or educational use. For details, contact:
DK Publishing Special Markets
1745 Broadway, 20th Floor, New York, NY 10019
SpecialSales@dk.com

Printed and bound in China

For the curious
www.dk.com